Justifying Ethics

Human Rights & Human Nature

JAN GORECKI

Justifying Ethics

Human Rights & Human Nature

Transaction Publishers
New Brunswick (U.S.A.) and London (U.K.)

Copyright © 1996 by Transaction Publishers, New Brunswick, New Jersey 08903.

All rights reserved under International and Pan-American Copyright Conventions. No part of this book may be reproduced or transmitted in any form or by any means, electronic or mechanical, including photocopy, recording, or any information storage and retrieval system, without prior permission in writing from the publisher. All inquiries should be addressed to Transaction Publishers, Rutgers—The State University, New Brunswick, New Jersey 08903.

This book is printed on acid-free paper that meets the American National Standard for Permanence of Paper for Printed Library Materials.

Library of Congress Catalog Number: 95-37865
ISBN: 1-56000-236-0
Printed in the United States of America

Library of Congress Cataloging-in-Publication Data

Górecki, Jan.
    Justifying ethics : human rights and human nature / Jan Górecki.
        p. cm.
    Includes bibliographical references and index.
    ISBN 1-56000-236-0 (alk. paper)
    1. Social ethics. 2. Human rights. I. Title.
HM216.G574   1995
177—dc20   95-37865
                                                                CIP

To Maria and Piotr

Acknowledgments

Major parts of four articles of mine reprinted here appeared first in the following places and are reproduced by the kind permission of the original publishers:

1. "Human Rights: Explaining the Power of a Moral and Legal Idea," 32. *The American Journal of Jurisprudence* 1987: 153-69.

2. "Human Nature and Justification of Human Rights", 34. *The American Journal of Jurisprudence* 1989: 43-60.

3. "Moral Norms: The Problem of Justification Reconsidered," *The Journal of Value Inquiry* 25: 349-58, 1991. © Kluwer Academic Publishers.

4. "Functionalism and Justification of Ethics" in *Laws and Rights* (Seminario Giuridico della Universita di Bologna, Misc. 10), Vincenzo Ferrari ed., Milano: Giuffrè 1991: 589-612.

Contents

Preface

The idea of human rights is powerful. An insight into its psychological and then its political power provides the best point of departure for the scrutiny of the questions explored in this book. This explains the contents of the introduction.

But, whatever its power, is the idea of human rights justified? More specifically, are the norms proclaiming human rights objectively justified or only subjectively experienced by their utterers? This question (relevant to all kinds of moral judgments) is forcefully contested by moral skeptics and their opponents.

The expression "objective justification" is vague. However, from the words of those who have tried to justify the norms they utter, a meaning of sufficient clarity can be derived. When claiming objective justification of a moral norm, they go beyond their feelings. They refer to the occurrence of an outside, nonpsychological fact "producing" the norm that, when believed to have occurred, compels us to accept the norm. I call it a "normmaking fact."

Several kinds of normmaking facts have played a major role in the history of ethical thought. The most influential of them is human nature. Some moral norms are claimed to either conform with the demands of, or be ingrained in, human nature; thus, our own nature compels us to accept them. Other frequently claimed kinds include the fact that the norm has been stipulated by a heteronomous, authoritative source, such as God or social contract, that the norm is a necessary dictate of reason, or that it is simply true.

In chapter 1, these considerations pave the way toward my inquiry into the problem of justification: the validity of at least some claimed justifications can be determined in a publicly convincing manner. Thus, we can discard any justification on analytical grounds if its logic is defective. We can also discard any justification by demonstrating that, even for those who accept the occurrence of the claimed normmaking fact, it is easy to reject the norms "produced" by it; that is, by demonstrating that the normmaking fact does not have compelling force. And, if the occurrence of a claimed normmaking fact is empirically testable, we may be able to test the justification.

In chapters 2 and 3 I apply this kind of examination to each of the major claimed normmaking facts, first and foremost to human nature. In the view of most thinkers, human nature denotes dynamic tendencies embedded in human physiology, mind, and social behavior. Thus understood, human nature can be partially reduced to its observable indicators. Two such indicators have emerged in scholarly debates. One is the universal human needs and wants. The other is the basic ethical inclinations expressed in universally accepted norms. There is also one more testable meaning in which human nature has been used for justification: owing to peculiarities of human nature, morality is with us to perform a specific function, and this compels us to accept the moral norms that serve the function well. These assertions have found strong support in many quarters—among anthropologists, psychologists, sociobiologists and philosophers. My scrutiny of the supporters' views refutes the claim that human nature, in whichever of these understandings, provides objective justification of human rights norms. This refutation is a step toward the stand of moral skeptics.

My inquiry then moves on to such claimed normmaking facts as divine will, Kantian reason, and the truth value of moral judgments. Their occurrence is not empirically testable, but the validity of some of them can be examined on the grounds of the two other criteria—their logic and, especially, their compelling power. Confronted with these criteria, some of the untestable justifications fail. And, since the compelling power of all the untestable justifications is historically variable, all of them may fail one day. This would vindicate the view of moral skeptics. However, even if such vindication were to occur, it would not be final.

My scrutiny can be forcefully challenged, and the challenge is addressed in chapter 4. Clearly, human nature, at least as specified here, does not justify human rights. However, human nature is a source of hope; due to a peculiar, empirical characteristic of human nature, the idea of human rights can be universally accepted by all nations and all governments as well. This characteristic consists in human polymorphism. Owing to this characteristic, the implementation of human rights can successfully occur, irrespective of whether they are objectively justified. Which easily raises a criticism of the perennial search for justification: the search is not really important and may well be forgotten. We ought to do what is right if doing so is feasible rather than to speculate why doing so is right.

Whatever its strength, this criticism cannot be accepted. As chapter 5 shows, objective justification is important and so is the search for it. The importance of justification is of two kinds, pragmatic and fundamental. The former comes from the enhancement of compelling force, that is, enhanced persuasiveness, of the ethical norms believed to be objectively justified. This enhancement constitutes, in turn, a major determinant of the wide acceptance of those norms. This determinant is badly needed by those who struggle for human rights. There are two basic components of their struggle. One is the action aiming at moral "contagion" of the people by the human rights experience. The other is taking the road from moral acceptance to legal implementation. Both of them suffer from overwhelming impediments, and a well-established objective justification cannot but help in overcoming the difficulty of the struggle.

But more than teleology is at stake here. The problem of justification is among the few most basic questions dealing with the ultimate nature and meaning of the world and the human condition. The answers to these questions have for us a fundamental, nonteleological value—an issue to which I return at the end of the book.

Let me precede my search with a few words dealing with its logic and its limitations. We happen to live in a time of acute epistemic and methodological conflict in the academic world, and the divide runs largely between the modern heirs of the Enlightenment and, broadly speaking, various kinds of postmodernists who challenge the worth of reason and objective knowledge.[1] That is why it is important to assert where this inquiry belongs. Basically, with one major reservation, it belongs to the modern, not postmodern intellectual tradition.

It does so because reason is a critical human adaptive implement, and so is its unique product known as scientific knowledge; their proper use constitutes today the best source of hope for the human future. (I speak here of the "proper use" only, since much scientific knowledge can be applied in both beneficial and deadly industrial or social technologies.) Accordingly, this inquiry accepts rationalism (understood as negation of antirationalism, not of empiricism), and it accepts experience as a vital source of objective knowledge. It accepts the classical, correspondence understanding of truth, and the testability of propositions as the demarcation line between scientific knowledge and metaphysics. (However, and this is the major reservation mentioned earlier, it rejects the positivist, especially neopositivist disregard for metaphysics. Generated by deep existential anxieties and hopes, the perennial quest after ultimate secrets of the world and human condition has always been, for most humans, an issue of paramount importance. That is why the quest deserves the utmost respect, even though it may be untestable forever.) Furthermore, this inquiry accepts the logical (but not causal) is/ought barrier. It also cherishes good logic, clarity, parsimony and, whenever feasible, simplicity of scholarly language.

Postmodern thought has been criticized by many writers, and it is not my purpose to join the critics or to volunteer a general evaluation of postmodernism; such an evaluation would require a major study scrutinizing, in a balanced way, all the merits and demerits of the doctrine. What I am doing now is dealing with one objection that should help to explain why this book belongs where it does. My only grievance against postmodern thinkers is their acceptance of truth relativism and, thus, their rejection of objective knowledge. Most of them are pragmatists. But theirs is not an innocent, commonsense pragmatic approach to knowledge—the conviction that "knowledge is chiefly to be valued as a guide to action."[2] Theirs is truth pragmatism—they identify the veracity of a proposition with its variably understood expediency, very often political expediency.[3]

Needless to say, that expediency is in frequent conflict with classically understood truth. And here the doctrine is harmful. When encountering contradiction between a classically true and an expedient proposition, a truth pragmatist tends to accept the latter one as true. So do the postmodernists, and to disguise the rejection of objective truth (which most humans cherish), some of them play games with language and logic.[4]

This is a dangerous method. First, it undermines scientific knowledge. And, by providing an ostensibly scientific justification of expedient politics and policies, it opens the door to political abuse. History is rich with instances of such abuse, even though committed under names and ideologies other than postmodernism. The Nazi construction of politically expedient genetics is one of them, and the Stalinist construction of Lysenko's genetics (within a more general demolition of biology and chemistry) is another one; the former brought about the Nazi horrors, and the latter—the near extinction of most of Soviet science and death of those scientists who dared, like Giordano Bruno over three centuries earlier, to defend the search for objective truth.[5]

In the United States and other liberal democracies, the postmodern truth pragmatism is, of course, not deadly. Nonetheless, its dangers are serious. Their seriousness depends upon the degree of testability of the discipline under attack. Thus, physics is on the safest grounds; even under Stalin, with chemistry and biology decimated, theoretical physics survived. And, as of today, neither chemistry nor biology seem to be endangered in academia. In the recently published words of two opponents of postmodernism, "the probability that science will sooner or later take [postmodern] critiques sufficiently to heart to change its fundamental way of knowing is vanishingly small."[6] On the other hand, however, the disciplines at a lower level of testability have been increasingly undermined. This is particularly true of social science—sociology, social psychology, sociology of law and legal theory, anthropology and political science, as well as of humanities, especially history. If their decline continues, the harm may be incalculable, not just for the future of the universities, but for the world at large. Today's world does not suffer from underdevelopment of sciences and technology. Its sufferings, dangers, and immense problems come largely from the dramatic degree to which "technology has outdistanced culture,"[7] in particular the development of human intellect and social responsibility. That is why defending the integrity of the disciplines dealing with culture—the social sciences and humanities—is a most pressing order of the day.

So much for the logic of this inquiry. Now let me add a word about its limitations. Human rights has grown, especially since World War II, into an enormous scholarly area addressed by scores of disciplines. Obviously, the scope of this inquiry had to be limited. Thus, it has been conducted from one specific perspective as outlined in the preceding comments. Accordingly, this book runs, for the most part, across moral and political philosophy, social policy, psychology, jurisprudence, and international law, and it only touches peripherally on a few other areas, in particular on social history and economics, to clarify the cultural and economic prerequisites for human rights implementation.

This book is not a moralist's exercise in normative ethics; its chapters contain propositions rather than evaluative judgments, even though sometimes an evaluation could not be avoided. However, I owe the reader a confession: one evaluation gave rise to the very notion of this book. This is the ethical acceptance of the idea of human rights and of the ongoing struggle for worldwide human rights implementation.

Having been shaped by a short list of moral principles, with the equal dignity of every human individual among them, the idea of human rights constitutes an invaluable product of Western civilization, its unique gift to all societies. Of course, the idea is rooted in the tradition of individualism. But here a clarification is needed. Disclaimers notwithstanding, the individualism that underlies the human rights idea does not entail egoism. As will be shown in chapter 5, the opposite is true. Human rights flourish not in societies of greedy egoists, but rather in societies of well-developed civic culture where the dominant attitudes include widely internalized obligations to respect the rights, liberties, and the well-being of others—at the workplace, in the family and community, and in public life in general.

My thanks are due to many persons. First, they go to all those who prepared me long ago, emotionally and intellectually, to deal with the subject of this book. Having been my teachers and then lifelong friends, they used openly and publicly the strength of their character and mind to defend human life and dignity against tyrannical rule. Most of them belonged to the great generation of the Warsaw-Lwow school of philosophy and, having survived World War II, remained in Poland after 1945. There were among them Tadeusz Kotarbiński, Jerzy Lande, Maria Ossowska, and Stanisław Ossowski. And there were also great thinkers of different philosophical persuasions, most remarkably Roman Ingarden, Antoni Kępiński, and Stanisław Stomma.

When writing this book I benefitted from help of many colleagues and friends. Those to whom I owe the most and in many ways are Walter Gellhorn, Gerald Gunther, Seymour Martin Lipset, David Riesman, and David S. Shwayder.

My wife, Danuta, a Byzantine scholar and a heroic figure during and after World War II (who for the "after" spent four years in political prisons in Cracow and Fordon) was an invaluable source of both supportive and critical comments. And so were our son Piotr and our daughter Maria.

The University of Illinois Department of Sociology was truly helpful in the preparation of the final version of the manuscript. For this I am indebted to Eva Ridenour and Monica Shoemaker, and, in particular, for the difficult computer work, to Gina Manning.

Last but not least, my thanks go to the truly dedicated and congenial house of Transaction Publishers. Working with Irving Louis Horowitz, Mary E. Curtis, Alicja Garbie was a rewarding experience. And special thanks are due to Laurence Mintz for his excellent editorial assistance.

Notes

1. This challenge is one important common characteristic of the otherwise eclectic body of postmodernists. The body includes, in particular, philosophical truth relativists operating in various areas, among them cultural constructivists in cultural anthropology, ethnography, sociology, and social history, deconstructionists and poststructuralists in literary and linguistic analysis, critical rhetoricians in communications studies, and many critical legal theorists, legal sociologists, and criminologists.
2. Ayer 1984: 102.
3. Many of them do so on the ground of epistemological skepticism; they assert the unknowability of the real world, and thus claim that factual propositions accepted by various groups are not descriptions of reality but socially determined mental constructions, all of them equally true even if they contradict each other. And which propositions does each group accept? It accepts those that are expedient for that group, that is, for a given culture, nation, class, or other interest group. Having asserted that, various brands of postmodernists consider the assertion particularly true (and here, "true" means classically true!) for one subculture which they have targeted for their search. This subculture is the modern academic world. Thus, according to the postmodernists, members of various disciplines within academia manufacture and accept only pragmatically true factual and explanatory propositions—that is, those expedient for themselves (and their partners), and, indirectly, for their benefactors who wield political and economic power.
4. The games consist in the use of flowery neologisms, metaphors, veiled truisms, and tautologies (sometimes used to smuggle in evaluative judgments). This style, first conceived in France has spread in other European countries and, in particular, in North America.
5. Many of its critics (most recently Gross and Levitt, 1994) stress that postmodernism is largely a product of the radically leftist political orientation. This is both true and interesting as a political fact. (For its explanation see Horowitz, 1993 *passim*, esp. pp. 48–49.) However, from the standpoint of scientific knowledge it does not matter whether a researcher is a leftist or a rightist. The ultimate bottom line of sound scholarship is whether a scholar's political views, whatever they are, do not subvert the search for objective truth, or, in Ernest Gellner's words, "the only possible shared idiom in terms of which paradigms could be compared and ranked in merit, would be reality itself: the paradigm closer to reality would then, naturally, be the better one" (Gellner 1992: 114).
6. Gross and Levitt, 1994: 236.
7. I owe this expression to Jan Steczkowski.

Introduction: The Power of Human Rights

"About the year 1774 a certain Thomas Paine arrived in Philadelphia from England with a letter of recommendation from Dr. Franklin," writes Benjamin Rush in his memoirs.[1] "In one of my visits to Mr. Aitken's bookstore I met with Mr. Paine, and...perceived with pleasure that he had realized the independence of the American Colonies from Great Britain...I asked him what he thought of writing a pamphlet upon it.... He readily asserted to the proposal, and from time to time...read to me [the emerging chapters]. I recollect being charmed with a sentence in it:... 'Nothing can be conceived of more absurd than three million of people flocking to the American shore every time a vessel arrives from England, to know what portion of liberty they shall enjoy.'"[2]

The product was *Common Sense*—a powerful appeal for parting from England in the name of political liberty, and that liberty was understood as a series of political rights, especially the equal right of everyone to a constitutional government representative of all; subsequently, Paine elaborated on this in *The Rights of Man. Common Sense* was followed, in the Declaration of Independence, by the claim "that all men are created equal, that they are endowed...with certain unalienable rights, that among these are life, liberty and the pursuit of happiness. That to secure these rights governments are instituted among men, deriving their just powers from the consent of the governed, [t]hat whenever any form of government becomes destructive of these ends, it is the right of the people to alter or to abolish it." Thirteen years later the National Assembly of France declared that "Men are born and always remain free and equal in their rights; [that] [T]he end of all political association is the maintenance of the...rights of man, and these rights are liberty, property, security and resistance to oppression; [that] [T]he nation is the...source of all sovereignty [and no one is] entitled to any authority unless it derives explicitly from the nation."[3] And, well over a century later,[4] at the other end of Europe, the Bloody Sunday petition was

1

addressed to the Tsar: "We, the workers of Saint Petersburg...have come to you, Sire, in search of justice.... We have fallen into poverty, we are oppressed, we are loaded with a crushing burden of toil, we are insulted, we are not recognized as men, we are treated as slaves... despotism and arbitrary law crush and strangle us...[We are] by aspect and appearance men. But in reality, we are not permitted any of a man's rights, not even the right of thinking, of meeting together, of examining our needs, of taking measures to better our lot. Whoever among us dares to raise his voice in defence of the rights of the working class is thrown in prison, is sent into exile...[We demand] the convocation of the representatives of Russia...[We demand] that the elections to a Constituent Assembly be carried out on the basis of universal, secret and equal suffrage. This is our most important demand; in and on it rests everything...[We also demand] liberty of speech, the press, meeting, and of conscience in religious matters..., equality before the law [and] release of all who have suffered for their convictions."[5] All these demands may sound commonplace in the America of today, but they did not sound so to contemporaries, in particular to the French of 1789 and the Russians of 1905.[6] Nor are they a commonplace for billions of those who live today under oppressive rule.

Historically, human rights originated from the doctrine of natural law. That doctrine, harking back to ancient and medieval thought, was, in its modern form, spelled out under the impact of Renaissance thought and the Protestant revolution. On its way from Grotius to Locke, the doctrine's focus shifted, from the ideal of a peaceful and secure domestic and international order, to the notion of the natural rights of the human individual. As articulated in the era of Enlightenment, the words "rights of man" denote individual rights against governmental oppression. In the name of a few principles protecting such fundamental values as human life, dignity, autonomy, and essential liberties, the rights of man are equally due to any man. Thus understood they include the right to freedom of thought, religion, speech and assembly, and to a fair system of criminal justice. But even in this basic political sense, the expression "rights of man," later transformed into "human rights," means different things in different historical contexts. In some societies, the struggle for these rights amounts largely to the pursuit of representative government; it was so conceived within the parliamentary history of England, and this pursuit was expressed forcefully in the

French Declaration, and then repeated by a range of manifestoes, from those of Lafayette in 1830 and Lamartine in 1848, to the faraway claims of the Decembrists in Russia and the more recent appeals by Sakharov. On other occasions, human rights demands have meant less than that. For instance, the stoics of imperial Rome—not so much human rights advocates as their forerunners—claimed human equality and alleviation of slavery, but not the abolition of despotic rule. Voltaire, when demanding religious and intellectual liberty and freedom from torture in criminal trials, hoped to enlighten, not remove the despots. Today as well, in societies at early stages of development, the human rights struggle aims at providing conditions for democracy rather than immediately instituting democratic systems.[7]

In still other contexts—at the opposite end of the political spectrum—human rights claims mean not just democracy, but more than that. The expanded meaning stems from the belief that not only despotic, but also representative government, can become oppressive, and, when this occurs, the citizen's rights provide a shield against the oppression. This perception first flickered in seventeenth-century British political thought; it can be traced through such early pronouncements as the Levellers' *appeale from the degenerate representative body,*[8] and Sir Edward Coke's famous dictum in *Regina v. Bonham.*[9] Finally, this perception has found its fullest expression in American constitutional doctrine where human rights represent "the majority's promise to the minorities that their dignity and equality will be respected."[10]

Beyond that a number of further social, economic, and cultural claims have been added to the already somewhat vague catalog in the decades following the World War II; the addition aimed at providing for greater socioeconomic equality and universal well-being. And, in recent years, a major effort has been made to add still another category to the growing and increasingly ambiguous list—various rights of collectivities, such as all peoples' right to development, self-determination, or peace.

Despite the ambiguity, the idea of human rights is appealing. It is a tenet prescribing claims against government. When pronounced in earnest,[11] it is expressive as well as instrumental; it expresses emotions of the speaker, and provides the audience with motivation for political behavior. Thus, it constitutes a linguistic utterance, a mental experience, and a stimulus for action. That is why, for its power to be fully understood, the idea must be submitted to socio-psychological examination, and, owing to the just noted historical determinants of its specific meaning, the idea must be put in historical perspective.

The Experience of Human Rights

We experience a variety of rights. Among them are moral and legal rights, rights generated by etiquette, by participation in games, and by membership in criminal gangs and social clubs. Human rights belong primarily to the first of these categories; they are moral rights.

What are the distinctive traits of moral rights? Moral rights are experienced as valid claims against others. These claims demand that the others do what they ought to do as right or refrain from doing what they ought to avoid as wrong; "right" and "wrong" means here right or wrong per se, without reference to any purposeful rationale. Human rights, experienced as valid claims in this sense, have two further peculiar characteristics: they are ascribed to all humans, and are directed at political powerholders. Sometimes—wherever positive law implements them—human rights become also legal rights. For instance, the rights proclaimed by the French Declaration of 1789 are, in France of today, both moral and legal. The same holds true of Tom Paine's claims under the American Constitution.

Let us take a closer look at moral rights in general. The experience of moral rights constitutes a peculiar kind of moral experience. Moral experiences emerge in us in response to ideas of (present, future, or past) acts that, according to one's system of evaluations, ought to be done as right or to be avoided as wrong. If the ideas are of present or future conduct, the moral feeling is the experience of a duty or of a corresponding right. If, on the other hand, the ideas are of the past and, moreover, of wrong conduct, the experience of the previously broken duty is known as "guilt"—a distressing feeling of one's own bad conscience and shame or of someone else's being guilty of wrongdoing. These feelings—of right, duty, guilt—have driving properties. In particular, the feeling of duty stimulates the demanded acts and inhibits the prohibited ones, whereas the feeling of rights stimulates steps to satisfy the claim.[12] (The feeling of guilt may also generate the driving experience of the duty to redress the wrong done,[13] and anticipation of a future bad conscience may arouse or reinforce an aversive drive against wrongdoing.[14]) Thus, what is discussed here is, basically, the morality of rights and duties. This understanding of morality, clear and useful for these considerations, leaves beyond the scope of this book some important traditional issues of moral discourse. There are among them supererogation, self-centered aspirations, and virtue and vice—the main focus of Aristotle's and today's Aristotelian moral philosophy.

We experience moral rights (and, for that matter, any rights) in one of two distinct ways—in the first person or as the rights of others. In the first person, moral rights appear as *my* rights against those duty-bound, for instance, my claim for alimony or my claim not to be searched without a warrant. Or, they may appear as *our* rights against those duty-bound. For instance, when undergoing or witnessing, in a liberal society, searches without a warrant or torture to elicit confession, each of us can experience such methods as infringements of our, that is, American (or French or British) rights, or rights due to us as civilized people, or rights due to us as human beings; in the last case we go through our human rights experience.

We can also experience moral rights as the rights of others. These rights may bind ourselves, and thus imply our own obligations; as a debtor, each of us can sense his creditor's rights. Or, if the rights of others imply obligations of someone else than ourselves, we often experience these rights "from the outside," as if we were observers.

Thus, when witnessing child abuse, we experience the child's rights against the abusive parent. When witnessing school segregation on the eve of *Brown v. Board of Education,*[15] many whites experienced (American or human) rights of the blacks against the school establishment. And, when learning about the more recent cruelties in Cambodia, Bosnia-Herzegovina, Haiti, or Chechnya, many people around the world have experienced human rights of the oppressed against their rulers.

Acquisition and Activation of the Experience of Rights

How do we acquire the experiences of rights? Or, more broadly, how do we acquire any moral experiences—our driving feelings of rights and duties, our reflective feelings of what is right and wrong, our embarrassing feelings of guilt and shame? We acquire them in the process of contagious social learning. The process operates through communications about what behavior is right and wrong, what one should and should not do, who can be proud of his acts and who should be ashamed.

The society in which we live "showers" each of us with these communications, and the communications "infect" us.[16] They come, for the most part, through the medium of language—spoken, written, sung. They come through gestures, facial expressions, examples, and other modeling influences, such as single, appealing acts, or the entire lifestyle of those whom we respect, especially our parents, peers, and reference individuals. Our peers, both in childhood and in adult life, are particularly influential here. Under the impact of their opinion many of us are inclined to believe in evidently false factual propositions,[17] not to speak of moral judgments, unavoidably more ambivalent than statements of fact. These communications often come in the form of reinforcement— punishments explicitly imposed for wrongdoing and rewards explicitly contingent upon acts evaluated as right.[18] They also come in such symbolic encounters as family, religious, or national ceremonies, and through various objects of arts.

This mechanism is responsible for the acquisition of moral experiences.[19] In the first place, it implants in the individual mind a system of evaluations—of convictions regarding what is right and wrong and what ought to be done and avoided. These evaluations are stored in our brain. They are internalized in both forms—as judgments on what is right and wrong, and as norms, that is, prescriptions about what ought to be done or avoided. The prescriptions can be articulated as an ought *due to* those entitled or as an ought *by* those duty bound; in the former articulation the norms pronounce rights, in the latter, duties. To be sure, this system of evaluations should be treated as a "system" in quotation marks only. In most of us it is vague, not genuinely thought through, often inconsistent, and never final.

When a specific, morally relevant stimulus occurs, the norms stored in our brain become activated. The "morally relevant stimulus" means here any stimulus producing the idea of an act which, according to one's system of evaluations, should be done as right or avoided as wrong; and the activation consists in arousal of the feeling of duty to behave accordingly or of the feeling of the corresponding right. Both feelings have energizing properties: they drive those duty bound to fulfill the experienced obligations, and they drive those experiencing their rights to pursue the claims.[20]

A few instances should make the issue clear. The morally relevant stimulus may consist in seeing a starving child, in discovering the opportunity to cheat on a tax return, or in being mistakenly convicted for an uncommitted crime. The person witnessing a starving child may previously have internalized such general norms as "help the needy" or "protect human life," or, having encountered or imagined a similar case before, he or she might have had internalized a more detailed norm, "rescue starving children." If one of these norms has been internalized already, it becomes easily activated now: witnessing a starving child arouses the feeling of duty to feed it. Similarly, in the second instance, if the taxpayer had internalized the norm "do not lie" or just "do not cheat on taxes," the idea of cheating arouses the feeling of the duty not to do so. And, in the last instance, if the convicted person's system of evaluations includes such norms as "one's freeedom should not be unjustly abridged," or a more detailed norm, "nobody innocent should ever be punished," the unfounded conviction arouses the feeling of the right to fight against the conviction and to have it quashed. In this manner, the internalized moral norms activate specific feelings of duty or right in concrete encounters.[21]

All this does not mean that our experiences of rights are always strong; on the contrary, most often they are not only weak, but they occur below the threshold of consciousness. Thus, when buying or selling in a smoothly operating market, we receive what is due nearly automatically without experiencing any excitement about our claims. When voting in a long-lived representative democracy, we do not strongly experience our right to vote (unless, perhaps, we have just reached voting age and vote for the first time). In an open society, when we go abroad or assemble for worship, there is no aroused sense about or even awareness of, our rights to do so. The same holds true for our experiences of duty. For the most part they are also weak if not subconscious; the majority of us do not steal or cheat and do pay debts virtually automatically.

What intensifies our feelings of rights and duties is counteraction and provocation. Counteraction consists of acts preventing rights from being implemented or duties from being fulfilled. Thus, if we buy any commodity, and the crooked seller, having received cash, refuses to deliver to us the item sold and claims "you didn't pay," our feeling of right to receive becomes clear and strong, and it may become overwhelming and stimulate action even on a sale of minor value. And, however weakly we experience our many common obligations, if someone counteracts them, for example, tries to persuade us to cheat, commit incest, or publicly ridicule the disability of a sick person, our feelings of a duty not to do so become powerful. Provocation, on the other hand, consists of any act (be this an act of counteraction or other behavior, such as vivid newspaper descriptions of someone's wrongdoing) performed deliberately to intensify our feelings of rights and duties.[22]

Counteraction and provocation by government evoke particularly strong emotions. Any American's experiences of rights, usually dormant, would become overwhelming if the government stopped him or her from voting, travelling abroad, assembling for worship, or exercising other constitutional rights. Indeed, various instances of governmental counteraction, or governmental acquiescence to counteraction by others, have occurred in the past—from racial discrimination in voting or occasional passport restrictions to the abuses of the McCarthy era. All of them resulted in an emotional arousal strong enough to either carry individual contests through federal courts[23] or to carry on major struggles through the entire political spectrum.[24] Of course, the counteraction is much more pronounced, and often reinforced by provocation, under despotic systems.

Rights against government are most frequently experienced in the first person, as "my" or "our" rights infringed upon. But, as hinted earlier, we also experience infringements of the rights of others; cruelties inflicted by autocrats abroad may arouse in us a clear feeling of rights of the victims (and of wrongdoing of the rulers), and generate action, from protests, through various kinds of indirect support, to participation in other peoples' wars and revolutions.[25]

Is the Language of Rights Nugatory?

As these comments indicate, we acquire moral experiences largely in the process of linguistic communications. But does this mean that, for the acquisition, the language of rights is truly necessary? There is a respectable moral and legal tradition that answers the question in the negative.

It follows from the very meaning of "right"—one's claim against someone else who should comply—that the experience of rights is always bilateral; anyone's right implies someone else's duty, and, thus, our feeling of X's right implies the feeling of Y's corresponding obligation. This implication gave rise to the view that the two expressions— "the right of X" and the corresponding "duty of Y" mean the same.

Consequently, we should, so the argument goes, forget about the language of rights, and replace it, without any change of meaning, by the simpler language of obligations. The debtor's duty would then replace the creditor's right; everybody's duty not to interfere would replace the owner's right to use his property; and the police duty not to search without a warrant would replace our rights against arbitrary searches. These replacements, both in moral and legal language, have been suggested by a line of thinkers from Pufendorf to Bentham to Kelsen.

The suggestion seems ill-advised. First, a right implies a corresponding duty, but the duty does not necessarily imply a right; consequently there is always a right-duty implication, but not always right-duty equivalence. To be sure, most often there is equivalence—duties without corresponding rights are a rare experience. Occasionally they do occur, however. For instance, those of us who experience the duty not to hurt animals rarely feel that rats or snakes have a right to be kindly treated.

Second, and more importantly, the right-duty equivalence that most often is present does not amount to right-duty synonymity. Sometimes those who use the expression "right of X" understand it plainly as the corresponding "duty of Y," and vice versa. Very often, however, this is not the case.

The two expressions are, indeed, synonymous for those looking "from the outside," without personal involvement, at the rights and corresponding duties of others, especially rights and duties of economic exchange. When we witness contracts and torts, and we perceive that Y is duty bound to pay rent or damages to X, Y's duty to pay means for us X's right to receive. This is how, particularly in civil cases, most judges experience the rights and duties of the parties involved.

The right-duty synonymity largely disappears, however, with respect to rights experienced in the first person. Whenever we sense them strongly, our experiences of our rights differ from our experiences of the corresponding duties of others; then the words "right" and "duty," even though equivalent, do not mean the same. In particular, our feeling of our rights—be they political, family, or economic—provides for our dignity, freedom, and economic sovereignty. In words spelled out nearly a century ago, in a largely unfree society, "Feelings of his (or her) right makes of a human an equal [to anyone else] in the relevant area...bestows on him personality of 'a citizen,' provides him with awareness of his dignity and self-respect...[makes] his posture erect, his head high, his voice determined."[26] And, in a strikingly similar view of a current American writer, "Having rights enables us to 'stand up like men,' to look others in the eye, and to feel in some fundamental way the equal of anyone. To think of oneself as the holder of rights is...to have...self-respect."[27] On the other hand, our feeling of the corresponding obligation of others refers to them rather than to ourselves; when experiencing their obligation, we feel what they ought to do or to avoid doing. If they do not comply, not only does this feeling intensify, but it often turns into a feeling of their wrongdoing and then into indignation, anger, even hatred. In this sense, anyone's experience of his right clearly differs from his experience of the corresponding duty.

We can observe the difference in everyday life. When someone illegally evicts us from our house, we go through both experiences with the stress shifting easily from one to the other: "This is my property; this is my home; I am the owner." But also: "How could anyone have done anything like that; how did he dare; what a rascal; he will pay for it."

We can also observe this difference in major social upheavals. Poland provides a relatively recent instance where the difference was observable on television thoughout the world. And, in contrast with the subsequent Eastern European revolutions, it was observable for several years, that is, long enough for the difference to be clearly visible. Solidarity was born in 1980 in the name of human and workers' rights. It emerged in the wake of the post-Helsinki spread of the human rights idea—a notion particularly appealing in that part of the world. Its emergence was precipitated by activities of dissident groups defending human rights and rights of labor, and, finally, by powerful utterances of John Paul II who, on his 1979 visit to Poland, repeatedly stressed human and workers' rights.[28] Consequently, the emotions of rights and dignity were clearly displayed by the posture, exclamations, and songs of millions during both papal visits—in 1979 and 1983. But there was also, especially after the imposition of martial law in December of 1981, a strong and widespread undercurrent of contempt, anger, and hatred against the commonly experienced wrongdoing of the powerholders. And, as in any revolutionary setting, it was easy for individuals and crowds to shift, in particular in response to provocation, from the dignified experience of "our" rights to the atmosphere of the hateful experience of "their" unmet obligations.

The same holds true with respect to all revolutions, wars perceived as "just," uprisings, and national liberation movements; the experience of one's own rights differs from that of the corresponding wrongdoing of governments or enemies. Characteristically, the American Declaration of Independence reflects this distinction—it first proclaims the rights of the Americans and only then turns to the long list of "repeated injuries and usurpations" by the King of Great Britain.

Thus, both in the private and public area—in the economic market and in political encounters—it is not true that we experience our rights as if they were corresponding obligations. This is why there is no general right-duty synonymity. The word "right" has an irreducible, stimulating sense, and the claim that we could replace the language of rights with the language of duties, and still make all our moral utterances without changing their meaning, is unfounded.

The Limitations and the Power of Human Rights

The preceding comments show how each of us acquires moral evaluations from those around us, and how, being activated, the evaluations stimulate behavior. This process does not determine, however, *which* moral evaluations the majority of us acquire. The evaluations expressed by members of any social group vary, and even in a well-integrated society many of them are in conflict. For example, should women be equally treated in the labor market and in access to political power? Should abortion be easily accessible, or never, or only occasionally? Should the traditionally underpriviledged be given equal or more than equal access to scarce goods? Every society becomes a large, ongoing "referendum" of evaluations. Some evaluations win the referendum in the process of communications and are accepted by the majority, while others tend to disappear.

Whether a moral norm wins or loses the referendum depends largely on a complex set of social and ecological conditions; the conditions differ from one pair of conflicting norms to another. For example, acceptance or rejection of the norms proclaiming equality of women depends on such characteristics of the society as the accepted rules of descent and inheritance, the type of economy and level of economic development, the class structure, the intellectual climate, and the degree of social mobility. Acceptance or rejection of various froms of birth control depends, among other factors, on the society's density of population and mortality rates, on the availability of food and other resources, parental expectations of children's achievement, and the religious tradition. Acceptance or rejection of the-more-than equal opportunity for the underprivileged depends, among other factors, on the society's political system and its stability, the relative number of the underprivileged, the level of education of all relevant groups, and the availability of economic resources.

This view applies specifically to human rights norms; lists of conditions for the acceptance of human rights norms differ from one norm to another. For instance, there are varying sets of conditions for the social acceptance of everyone's right to equal opportunity, to freedom of religion, to economic benefits specified in the United Nations covenants, or to a democratic government. Accordingly, it would be difficult to expect the social acceptance of equal rights for all in a tradition-oriented caste society or of the right to freedom of religion in a well-established theocracy. And it would be difficult to demand in earnest everyone's right to a high standard of living in a sub-Saharan tribe or everyone's right to democracy in the Athens of Draco.[29] Clearly, nobody can reasonably expect or demand the impossible. Thus, for each human right, the conditions for social acceptance and implementation may be present in some and absent in other societies; which implies an important (and dangerous) historical limitation of the human rights idea—an issue to which I will return later.

Whatever its limitations, these considerations should clarify the role and the energizing force of the idea. For its proponents, this has been the idea of the fundamental value of the human person—of human life, liberty, and dignity, and for many of them also of human equality, and individual well-being. The proponents express the idea in normative language of individual rights against political powerholders. The lists of rights vary, from Locke's triad of life, liberty, and property to the long catalog of political and socioeconomic claims conceived by United Nations covenants.

Human rights proclamations are not only expressive, but also instrumental; like all proclamations of moral norms, they are "calculated...to arouse feeling, and so to stimulate action."[30] The resulting arousal and stimulation should now be easy to explain. Such proclamations communicate to anyone what is due each of us and should thus be adhered to by those in political power. These communications become stored in the evaluative systems of those in the audience or they at least strengthen the norms already stored there. And, if the social conditions for their wide acceptance are present, these communications may win large enough numbers of individuals to become an ingredient of society's moral code. Then, in response to the morally relevant stimuli, the norms so internalized become activated in the minds of a multitude of people. And, if the stimuli consist in a major governmental counteraction or provocation, the thus aroused feelings of human rights may become overwhelming. This was exactly what happened in America following the "Intolerable Acts" of the British Parliament, in France following Louis XVI's response to the establishment of the National Assembly, and in Russia in the wake of the Bloody Sunday massacre of St. Petersburg workers. If not hampered by opposing influences, such as clearly prohibitive costs or hopelessness of the struggle, these feelings push those who experience them into social action, peaceful, violent, or revolutionary. This is how the human rights idea generates arousal and stimulates struggle in the name of what its proponents perceive as the intrinsic value of the human individual.

Notes

1. Corner 1948: 113-14.
2. This sentence was not published "by accident, or perhaps by design," *ibid.*
3. Sections I-III of the Declaration of Rights of Man and Citizen.
4. On January 22, 1905.
5. Postgate 1962: 363-65.
6. They certainly sounded stronger to the French of 1789 than the words of the Declaration of Independence to the Americans of 1776; on the eve of the French Revolution, the French had lived long under a genuinely despotic rule.
7. Cf. 96-98, 103, *infra.*
8. Tuck 1979: 149.
9. 77 Eng. Rep. 646 (1610).
10. Dworkin 1977: 205.
11. Like any great idea, this one can be declared in bad faith. Today, various autocrats pay lip service to it, and even democratic governments utilize human rights to challenge hostile, but not "friendly" tyrannies abroad. (However, for a qualification of this statement see chapter 5, note 10, *infra.*)
12. I basically accept here the most incisive sociopsychological analysis of the driving properties of rights and duties provided long ago by Petrażycki 1959 *passim*, and 1959-60, vol.1: 5-189. Today, various experimental studies tackle the issue. Studies of the feeling of duty to help another provide an instructive instance. They identify conditions that influence, in individual encounters, the emergence of the feeling of duty, its intensity, and its activating force. These conditions include the potential helper's perception of his own ability to help, his perception

of the need on the part of the recipient and of the need's significance, his estimate of the costs of help, and his apprehension of his peculiar, personal responsibility. For an excellent overview of these studies, see Schwartz 1977: 221-79; see also Schwartz and Howard 1981: 189-211. (For a review of studies of altruism conducted from a cost-reward perspective—many of them confusing moral with teleological motivation—see Dovidio 1984: 361-427).

13. For a summary of empirical evidence, see Walster, Berscheid, and Walster 1976: 1-42.

14. In this society, however, the feeling of duty, not the fear of guilt and shame, constitutes the primary motive against wrongdoing; in various inquiries, the fear correlated significantly with intended altruistic behavior, but "feelings of moral obligation were substantially better predictors" (S.H. Schwartz 1977: 240-41).

15. 247 U.S. 483 (1954).

16. The epidemiological model of morality (and other driving experiences) was elaborated first, in Darwinian manner, by Petrażycki 1959-60: 679-82; "Emotional Contagion," (written in Russian in 1912 and published posthumously) in Petrażycki 1985: 441-53. (For a similar model accepted much later, see Monod 1969: 16-17.) This perception of morality accepts "natural selection" of culture by process of learning, not through genetic change; those cultural traits, among them those moral experiences, which serve the adaptation of the group, tend to survive, whereas those that are dysfunctional tend to disappear. For reasons explicated later, in the chapter "The function of ethics," my use of the term "contagion" does not entail this kind of Darwinian stand.

17. See the famous experiment by Asch (1951: 177-90; 1952: 450-501), repeated by a number by follow-up studies.

18. Cf. Gorecki 1979: 17-27.

19. This has been, of course, only a very general description of the mechanism. The description disregards, for instance, the differential impact of age on the acquisition of moral experiences, and such cognitive influences as our knowledge and understanding of facts; I will return to these determinants later (on 85-86, *infra*). However important, the operation of these determinants does not undermine the validity of the basic tenet that we acquire moral experiences by being exposed to moral communications.

20. The idea of the internalized system (or, in his words, "structure") of evaluations and of its activation has been most precisely articulated by Schwartz 1977: 231ff. Schwartz's study, dealing with altruism (a subject of keen interest to an increasing number of experimentally oriented social psychologists) is relevant for all kinds of moral evaluations.

21. Here, however, an important reservation must be made. With our systems of evaluations loose and incomplete, each of us sometimes responds to a concrete encounter by a feeling of a "new" duty or right, that is, a duty or right irreducible to the already internalized norms. In this manner each of us can, in a new situation, articulate and accept a new norm "on the spot" and, while applying it to the case at hand, store it, within his or her system of evaluations, for future occasions.

22. The idea of counteraction and provocation has been, in a different context and slightly different manner, articulated by Petrażycki 1959-60, vol.1: 10-11, 46-49, 90-94.

23. Cf. *Kent v. Dulles*, 357 U.S. 116 (1958), and *Aptheker v. Secretary of State*, 378 U.S. 500 (1964), on passport restrictions. Voting rights infringements were dealt

with by a long line of court decisions, many of them summarized by Chief Justice Warren in *South Carolina v. Katzenbach*, 383 U.S. 301 (1966).

24. Various kinds of counteraction, sometimes amounting to provocation, brought about a powerful enhancement of the experience of black rights, among others, the right of blacks to vote. The enhancement was displayed in protests, demonstrations, marches, sit-ins, and the violence of the 1950s and 1960s. Civil rights legislation constituted an important response on the part of the Congress which, "confronted by an insidious and pervasive evil...concluded that the unsuccessful remedies which it had prescribed in the past would have to be replaced by sterner and more elaborate measures in order to satisfy the clear commands of the Fifteenth Amendment" (Chief Justice Warren in *South Carolina v. Katzenbach*, 383 U.S. 301 (1966). The counteractions of McCarthyism provoked enough emotional arousal—in particular in the media, the military, the executive branch, and among the lawmakers themselves—to prod the Senate to eliminate abuses and rectify the political process.

25. Such altruistic actions are, however, relatively rare; one reason for this is that our nervous system tends to defend itself from stimulus overload. The experience of others' broken rights is aversive. Vivid perception of any individual's suffering, especially of torture, degradation or killing, brings about grief on the part of the observer. Governmental cruelties have been perpetrated on millions of individuals the world over. This century brought the Holocaust. It also brought the Stalinist gulags, the slaughter of Armenians, Cambodians under Pol Pot, Ugandans under Amin, and the ruthless killing of a growing number of other ethnic groups in the 1990s. Being vividly informed about cruelties abroad constitutes a genuine overload of aversive stimuli. To avoid the grief (and the major loss of energy if driven to act), many people are inclined to insulate themselves by not knowing or not reacting. "When I have made myself read some of the literature on concentration (and labor) camps, I have been aware of my wish for mechanisms to put this terrible material at a distance," says Riesman (1964: 8). This inclination is reinforced by the feeling of helplessness due to lack of control over distant autocrats. (On the role of stimulus overload in other areas of altruistic behavior, see, e.g., Milgram 1970: 1461-68; Darley and Latane 1970.)

26. Petrażycki 1959-60, vol.1 206, 209, 210.

27. Feinberg 1970: 252.

28. Solidarity was both a social revolution and a national uprising, and it would be difficult to overestimate the impact of the Catholic Church and of the Pope on its emergence in 1980 and its triumph in 1989-1990; which, of course, does not necessarily mean that the subsequent concentration of power in the hands of the Church—the one and only religious organization of widespread influence—has been congenial to the development of new democratic institutions.

29. Cf. 94, *infra*.

30. Ayer 1950: 108. Originally spelled out in 1936, these words constituted, at that time, a new idea by an empirically oriented philosopher laying down foundations for the emotivist theory of values. The relevance of the theory for the sociopsychological inquiry of moral experience is obvious. Nonetheless, experimental social psychology of moral behavior of today seems either unaware of or unwilling to refer to the emotivist school.

1

The Problem of Justification

Would human rights advocates be at ease with the preceding analysis? The idea of human rights, like that of any other moral rights and duties, may seem to have been reduced here to individual experiences and their expressions—to the feelings of rights and to norms expressing those feelings. Thus understood, human rights norms, like all other moral norms, become subjective, personal pronouncements. This is exactly how moral skeptics perceive ethics. "There are no objective values," they assert.[1] Any moral judgment, especially a moral norm, is a product of its utterer's moral experience, and thus it does not express anything but the utterer's subjective state of mind. Because of their proximity to our minds or hearts—the skeptics maintain—the ultimate moral norms become the first principles that we consider so obviously binding that we accept them without any further evidence or explanation. We make them, we choose them, and their acceptance is "a responsibility that falls upon ourselves."[2] Thus, they become moral axioms from which lower-level norms can be deduced.

This subjectivist stand differs from how most of their advocates understand human rights norms. And, more inclusively, it differs from how most of their utterers understand any moral norms. For instance, a parent's or a preacher's utterance "you shouldn't steal," if conceived as a moral norm,[3] expresses much more than the utterer's personal feeling (however strong the personal feeling may be). The utterance means that you should not kill in the most objective manner, independently of the parent's or the preacher's personal opinion. And the words of the Declaration of Independence did not mean that all men have inalienable rights to "life, liberty and the pursuit of happiness" because I, Mr. Thomas Jefferson, or we, the members of the Continental Congress, feel so; what Jefferson and the other signatories of the Declaration said meant that every man has these rights objectively, independently of anyone's personal views. That is, they claimed that the validity of human rights norms is not just subjectively experienced, but objectively justified. And so is, in the view of any utterers, the validity of other moral norms.

But may this claim be accepted? Does not our feeling of the objective, "binding" force of moral norms constitute an illusion, a false claim "ingrained in our language and thought"?[4] In other words, can our moral utterances be objectively justified at all? This question—the problem of justification—has proved intractable enough to be sometimes quietly passed over. Still, it is often perceived as a crucial question for normative ethics, especially for the human rights idea.

It is clear why the question is significant. By dealing with the general view of the world and the human condition it has, for many of us, fundamental importance. Furthermore, it is intellectually perplexing: is the assertion of the objective validity of moral judgments true, or is it only a widespread illusion (to be feasibly registered among many other "pathetic fallacies" or Baconian *idola fori*)? The answer to this question has also practical implications. Utterers of any moral norms want themselves to be sure they have strong reasons for the acceptance of the norms they cherish. And, most importantly, they want those norms to be accepted by the society they live in, or even by all societies. Convincing reasons help this acceptance. But the utterer's subjective feelings can hardly be perceived as a convincing reason; only objective grounds are truly instrumental for persuasion.[5] Thus, objective justification constitutes a major determinant of the wide acceptance of the norms they utter. That is why the search for objective justification of ethics has lasted for over two thousand years, and is often perceived as the "most important...problem of philosophical ethics."[6]

To answer the question of justification, one must first determine the meaning of "objective justification." To be sure, grievances have been made about the vagueness of the expression: "Hardly any...moral philosophers...give any clear idea of how they are using the terms 'objective' and 'subjective.'"[7] However, from the viewpoint of most of those who have tried to justify the norms they utter, a meaning of sufficient clarity does emerge. As I noted in the preface, when claiming objective justification of a moral norm, they go beyond their own feelings. They refer to the occurrence of an outside, nonpsychological (and, in this sense, objective) fact "producing" the norm that, when believed to have occurred, compels us to accept the norm. I will call it a "normmaking fact." The full list of normmaking facts ever suggested, by anyone anywhere, would be long and largely queer. Thus, I will deal here only with those kinds of normmaking facts that have played a major role in the history of ethical thought.[8]

The first, and by far most influential of them, is human nature: some moral norms are claimed to either conform with demands of, or be ingrained in, human nature; thus, our own nature compels us to accept them. This kind of justification has been with us since the Socratics. The function of ethics constitutes here one important subdivision: owing to peculiarities of human nature, morality is with (or in) us to perform a specific function, and this compels us to accept the norms that serve the function well. A very different, frequently claimed kind of normmaking fact is that the norm has been stipulated by a heteronomous, authoritative "source," such as God or social contract. This is how many theists of various creeds, some natural law advocates, and some social contractarians understand justification of the norms they utter. Another kind is that the norm is a necessary dictate of reason; in the Kantian view, particularly influential within this tradition, reason means here pure, *a priori* reason of any existing or imaginable rational being. And still another kind is that the norm is, simply, true. More precisely, things as they are (or the world as it is) become here the normmaking fact, and the norm only reports them, as any true statement of fact does. Once norms such as "you should not kill" or "all humans have inalienable rights" are established as true, their veracity compels us to accept the norms. In other words, acceptance of the norms is here as objectively justified as that of any true statement of fact. This is how cognitivists—ontological idealists and modern intuitionists—understand the justification.

One reservation must be added here: there is one kind of reasoning obviously excluded from the above list of feasible justifications. This is a moral norm's reduction to a more general norm within the same system of primary norms.[9] The reduced norm's entailment may be simple: "you should not lie on tax returns" is simply entailed by the more general norm "you should not lie." Most often, however, the entailment is due to a conjunction of the more general norm with a factual statement about the consequences of behavior prescribed or proscribed by the norm to be justified. For instance, the norm "you should not lie on tax returns" may be reduced to a more general norm, "do not endanger the society's survival," with the addition of a factual premise that cheating on taxes endangers survival of the society. Or, such norms as, "you should not maim others" or "you should not degrade others" or "you should feed the hungry" may be reduced to the more general norms, "do not inflict suffering" or "do maximize happiness," with the addition of a factual premise that maiming or degrading or nonfeeding of the hungry brings about increase of suffering or decrease of happiness. This is how consequentialists, especially utilitarians, justify specific moral norms they utter. Reduction of this kind, sometimes called "internal justification," constitutes an entirely legitimate procedure. However, for obvious reasons, it is excluded from the above list of the feasible objective justifications: it consists in moving, within the same primary system, from less to more general norms, until we reach the most general (or "ultimate" or "basic") norm or norms of the system, with the problem of their justification, again, unresolved.

The compelling force of any normmaking fact always comes from the acceptance of a relevant rule of recognition. Any normative system, moral or legal, can be limited to primary norms which stipulate the contents of the prescribed or proscribed behavior. Or, it can be understood more broadly, to also include a rule of recognition of primary norms, that is, a rule which orders the general acceptance of the whole category of primary norms.[10] For instance, pronouncement such as "we accept true statements" or "we should obey norms ingrained in human nature" or "we should obey orders of God," are the rules of recognition of any true norms, or norms ingrained in our nature or issued by God. (As these instances indicate, the rules of recognition are a linguistic mixture. The pronouncement "we accept true statements" is a statement of fact. The provision "we should obey orders of God" is a norm. And the assertion "we must obey norms ingrained in human nature" can be understood as either a norm meaning that we ought to obey, or an implicit teleological proposition meaning that we cannot help but to obey, since otherwise we would bring about impossible consequences.)

Of course, the compelling force of various rules of recognition is uneven. Accordingly, the compelling force of various normmaking facts is also uneven. Thus, some suggested justifications are stronger than others. In particular, some normmaking facts, if believed to have occurred, make the acceptance of the norm a self-evident must; the way our mind works makes the rejection of the norm hardly conceivable. One rule of recognition is exceptionally strong; the way our mind works makes its rejection virtually impossible. This is the rule "we accept true statements"; its acceptance sounds like a self-evident must. Consequently, rejection of a moral norm believed true is hardly conceivable.[11] (This is probably why some moral thinkers, when speaking of objective justification, have in mind only the question of the truth value of moral judgments.) On the other hand, most, if not all, other rules of recognition have only persuasive power, and the degree of their persuasiveness varies. This is, for instance, the case with such rules as "we should obey orders of God" or "we should obey social contract." Accordingly, the conviction that a moral norm was imposed by God or social contract can only, more or less forcefully, persuade those convinced to accept the norm. To justify a moral norm in the sense accepted here, the force of the normmaking fact must be genuine: for those who are convinced that the normmaking fact did occur, it must be difficult (if at all possible) to reject the norm.

Thus, the logic of the justifying reasoning should be clear by now; this is a syllogism, with the rule of recognition as the large premise, the statement of normmaking fact as the small one, and the norm to be justified as conclusion. Sometimes, whenever both premises and the conclusion are statements of fact, the syllogism is classical; this is the case when the veracity of a norm is claimed as the normmaking fact. More often, the syllogism is practical, moving from a normative large premise to a normative conclusion. Clearly, this reasoning is not tainted by naturalistic fallacy—it never moves from an "is" in both premises to an "ought" in the conclusion.

One further comment must be added here. The compelling force of any rule of recognition is not entirely independent of the contents of the moral norms it is claimed to justify. The dependence may be of two kinds. First, a rule of recognition can lose its force if the moral norms it is claimed to justify run strongly against the society's moral intuitions. For instance, had social contractarians claimed that the original social contract stipulated slavery, the rule of recognition, "we should follow the social contract," would not be persuasive in a liberal society. And, second, a rule of recognition can lose its force if the moral norms it is claimed to justify are clearly irrelevant for the society's intuitions. For instance (to paraphrase a well- known example by Philippa Foot[12]) had social contractarians claimed that the original social contract stipulates everone's duty to clasp hands three times an hour, the contractarian rule of recognition would lose its persuasiveness as well.[13] Thus, there is a degree of "circularity" (that is, two-way adjustment) in the justifying reasoning. This kind of circularity is not unusual in the reasoning of analysts of normative systems—it resembles the "reflective equilibrium" idea of some moral thinkers,[14] and the "hermeneutical circle" in legal reasoning.[15]

These comments may pave the way toward the resolution of the problem of justification. As they imply, the validity of at least some claimed justifications can be assessed in a publicly convincing manner. Of course, we can rebut any attempted justification on analytical grounds if its logic is defective. We can also rebut any attempted justification by demonstrating that, even for those who accept the occurrence of the claimed normmaking fact, it is easy to reject the norms "produced" by it, or, in other words, that the rule of recognition is not persuasive. And, if the occurrence of a claimed normmaking fact happens to be empirically testable, we may be able to test the justification and to feasibly refute it by disproving that the normmaking fact has occurred (e.g., by disproving that there ever was a social contract.[16]) These steps can be applied to the various kinds of normmaking facts just listed and bring either rebuttal or corroboration of the proposed justifications. The corroboration of at least one would provide us with objective justification of ethics and, especially, of human rights norms, whereas the rebuttal of all would support the stand of moral skeptics. This kind of scrutiny will be conducted now, starting with human nature as justification, and then moving beyond human nature.

Notes

1. This is the well known sentence opening the first chapter of J.L. Mackie's book (1977: 15).
2. Ayer 1984: 34. Cf. also Popper 1971, vol.1: pp. 62–66.
3. Of course, this utterance may be conceived as a nonmoral prescription. In particular, in some contexts it may express an aesthetic rather than a moral aversion against stealing; in others, it constitutes a teleological demand, e.g., when "you shouldn't steal" implies "to avoid punishment" or "to be respected."
4. Mackie 1977: 35, 48–49.
5. For a qualification of this view see 135, note 1, *infra*.
6. Gewirth 1978: ix.
7. Hare 1981: 206.

8. For a few instances of normmaking facts claimed in the past and omitted here see 67–68, *infra*.
9. On the meaning of "primary system" see the following paragraph.
10. The expressions "primary" norms and "rules of recognition" have been used, in a different meaning, by Hart 1961, *passim*, esp. chapter 5.
11. A qualification must be added here, however. First, and quite obviously so, the fact that we intellectually accept true statements does not imply that we always admit their acceptance; otherwise, there would be no liars. And, moreover, those in a pathological state of mind are sometimes unable to face and thus to intellectually accept the truth.
12. Foot 1978: 111, 118, 119.
13. That is, the rule would lose its persuasiveness, unless some factual background information made the claim relevant.
14. This Socratic idea has been most consistently developed by Rawls 1971: 20, 48–51.
15. Cf., e.g., Larenz 1983: 197–202; Peczenik 1983: 81–82. Cf. also Hare's idea of testing normative deductions from a moral principle "by following out their consequences" and seeing whether we can accept the consequences, and, subsequently, the principle itself; which would be done in a manner analogous to "the Popperian theory of scientific knowledge" (1963: 91, 92).
16. Social contract has often served, from Hobbes to Rawls, as a useful philosophical fiction. However, to be experienced as binding, social contract must be understood as a genuine historical fact.

2

Human Nature

The idea of nature has a powerful appeal; when we discover that nature compels us to do something, most of us feel strongly pressed and are easily persuaded to follow.[1] That is why, for those who perceive it as the mainspring of any norm, nature constitutes a justification of the norm in the sense accepted here. And indeed, nature has been widely used as a justifying device for moral norms. It has also been used as a justifying device for legal norms by various doctrines of natural law, thus endowing these norms with more than government-imposed validity (and providing an ultimate criterion of validity for entire systems of positive law.)

But does nature, and in particular human nature, prescribe or proscribe behavior? Those who claim that it does, use the expression "human nature" in a variety of rather vague meanings. Thus, its clear sense must be stipulated before human nature can be assessed for justification.

According to most thinkers, "human nature" denotes dynamic tendencies ingrained (by divine, cosmic, biological or social forces) in human physiology, mind, and social behavior. To be sure, so understood, the notion is still vague enough. However, it is not necessarily void of sound empirical sense, and so is not irreparably vague. It can be used as a theoretical construct similar to notions such as human "personality," or "bio-psychological traits." Thus conceived, human nature can be partially reduced to its observable indicators. Two such indicators have emerged in the history of moral thought. One of them is the universal human needs and wants. The other is the basic ethical inclinations expressed in universally accepted norms. I will deal with each of them in the comments to follow, then I will turn to human nature as understood by a long line of thinkers who have attempted to explain ethics by its function.

Universal Needs and Wants

Universal human needs and wants have often been used as a source of justification of moral demands. Those who claim that such needs and wants exist provide us with divergent catalogs. They list, first, physiological conditions necessary for the human organism to stay alive, develop, and reproduce. "Everybody requires the conditions for life and health, and most people require the conditions of biological survival," such as food, air, drink and shelter, claims Bertrand Russell.[2] Others add to the list rest, sex, and safety from physical injury.[3]

These lists are not limited to physiological necessities. Another condition for human survival is membership in society. This brings about the *appetitus societatis*—"a desire for a life spent...tranquilly...in common with fellow-men."[4] And since people in society "are driven to practice justice," the universal need for justice follows.[5] Other universal needs and wants that emerge from our social nature are believed to include love and affection, surcease of anxiety,[6] and, in particular, liberty, dignity,[7] self-respect.[8] From Democritus onward, the need for happiness—understood in a variety of ways, for instance as Aristotelian *eudaimonia*, as J. S. Mill's higher pleasures and absence of pain, or as sheer hedonism—has claimed to be universal. Modern thinkers have expanded the lists of items included, and subdivided them into further categories.[9]

Use of universal needs and wants as a source of justification of moral demands is frequent. The proponents of this use assert that since these needs and wants are part of our nature, we should enable everyone to satisfy them (or, at least, not prevent anyone from satisfying them). The meaning of this assertion is not entirely clear. Some of its proponents consider the assertion a logical inference; in their view, the statement that X is a universal need or want entails the moral rightnes of attaining X, and thus they commit the is-implies-ought fallacy.[10] But the majority of the proponents do not go that far. They simply feel that we must follow the necessities of human nature. Thus, they implicitly accept, as a major premise, the rule of recognition "we should enable everyone to satisfy the natural [that is, in operational terms, universal] human needs and wants." With the addition, as a minor premise, of the statement of normmaking fact "a, b, c are universal human needs and wants," the norm "we should enable everyone to satisfy a, b, c" follows. The minor premise is perceived as the objective justification for this norm.

How valid is this justification? According to the criteria of validity stipulated above, the minor premise provides a justification of the normative conclusion if this premise is true and persuasive, and if the logic of the justifying reasoning is correct. By avoiding the naturalistic fallacy, most proponents of this justification seem to be on safe logical grounds. But is the statement of the normmaking fact spelled out in the minor premise true and persuasive? In other words, are the supposed universal needs and wants just listed indeed universal? And if they are, how persuasive is their universal character?

The answer to these questions differs from one category of needs and wants to another. The needs and wants that are deemed to justify most human rights—the need of political liberty, individual growth, basic equality, and, in at least one important sense, dignity—can hardly be claimed universal. There are caste societies, as well as tradition-oriented, male-dominated societies, in which demand for equality is not widely experienced. There have been tradition-oriented authoritarian societies, such as Sparta, in which despotic rule does not arouse a yearning for free political institutions or for the fullest development of the human individual; and, if respect for human dignity is understood as equal treatment and liberty, the need for dignity is not widely experienced in those societies either. Also need for peaceful and friendly living together with other members of the human species is not universally experienced; human history has always been marked by enthusiasm for war, violence, and hatred as visibly as by the wish for peaceful and amicable life. Whether the need for happiness is so experienced is unclear, due to the indefiniteness of the term. And even the need for justice cannot be claimed universal. Demands for justice are voiced in many, if not all, societies, and that is why the need for justice is frequently believed to work everywhere. However, this universality is illusory. "Justice" is a formal ethical term, and thus its meanings abound. Because of its wide and shifting connotation, it often means different things in different social contexts.[11]

Thus, there seems to be only one category of needs and wants that is clearly universal; this is physiological human necessities. People in all societies, whenever deprived, go through such experiences as drive for food, water, air, physical activity, rest, reproduction, and protection from injury by other humans, animals, disease, or climate. Thus, with respect to these biological basics of human existence, the minor premise "a, b, c are universal human needs and wants" is obviously true.

There is a problem, however, with the persuasiveness of this premise, that is, with the compelling force of the underlying rule of recognition. Everybody everywhere knows: I need, and everyone else needs, food, water, protection from injury, and so on. But does this knowledge persuade everybody to accept the rule of recognition "we should give everyone, or at least not deprive anyone of, access to food, water, protection from injury"? To be sure, some of us are inclined to genuinely accept this norm. So are, for instance, the utilitarians. Maximizing human happiness (whatever it means), and minimizing suffering, constitutes the ultimate and universalized principle of their primary moral system; apparently, this principle entails the norm "we should do whatever is possible to enable every human to satisfy the basic human needs and wants," since the alternative produces misery. However, at least as yet, the utilitarians have not swayed the world.[12]

Accordingly, few societies translate universal biological human needs into universal human rights. Most societies, whenever immersed in internal or external wars, have gladly deprived their foes of the biological basics, with the result of immense suffering and widespread loss of life, sometimes of genocidal proportions. Thus, the minor premise "a, b, c are universal human needs and wants," even though known to be true to everyone, does not bring the general acceptance of the norm "we should enable everybody human to satisfy a, b, c." Since it is unpersuasive for most of those who know its veracity, the premise does not constitute a valid justification.[13] In other words, human nature, if reduced to universal human needs and wants, cannot be treated as objective justification of human rights norms.

Basic Ethical Inclinations: Universally Accepted Norms

The Universalist Tradition

The second of the two indicators of human nature is the basic ethical inclinations as expressed in the universally accepted norms. This indicator provides us, again, with a precise, empirical version of justification. The question whether there are moral norms ingrained in human nature becomes operational: are there any universally accepted moral norms? In particular, are there any universally accepted norms establishing human rights? There is an important intellectual tradition that answers these questions in the positive. The tradition can be traced back to ancient and, in particular, Renaissance thought.[14] In its contemporary form it comes from various areas of scientific knowledge—anthropology, psychology, sociobiology, as well as philosophy.

A few decades ago, some of the leading anthropologists reacted against the radical relativism dominant in their discipline. That relativism would pervade anthropology is understandable. The field workers had been impressed by the diversity of cultures and, especially, by the variation of moral norms from one society to another. They felt unable to find any norms universally approved. From this factual insight—the descriptive version of relativism—they moved to the acceptance of two further assertions. The first was a metaethical claim: objective justification of moral norms is impossible. The second was an evaluative judgment: moral norms of all societies are equally right; consequently, no one has grounds for challenging the norms of any alien society.[15]

Both assertions aroused critical reaction. The former provoked criticism by those inclined to justify at least some moral norms by their universal acceptance. The latter—of those who believe that it is right to challenge norms of other cultures, and that to maintain that "anything goes" in alien societies amounts to perversion of tolerance. To be sure, the former assertion is not necessarily implied by the acceptance of descriptive relativism, and the latter is an obvious non-sequitur.[16] However, since perception of the normative diversity easily generates both claims in the scholar's mind, especially in the mind of an anthropologist enamored of the societies under his or her scrutiny, the critical reaction turned against descriptive relativism itself. There was one more reason for turning against this version of relativism: its acceptance runs against the appealing idea of the ethical unity of the human species.

The critics refer to various ultimate moral norms they consider universally accepted; by universality they mean acceptance of the norms by overwhelming majorities in all societies, rather than unanimity of all individuals everywhere.[17] Various lists of the claimed "universals" include prohibitions of killing, maiming, and incest, duties arising from parenthood, property, and contracts, as well as the general duties of reciprocity and fair dealing.[18] There is here also approval of bravery, justice,[19] kindliness, sympathy, and regard for others and their rights.[20] "If, in spite of biological variation and historical and environmental diversities, we find these congruences, is there not a presumptive likelihood that these moral principles somehow correspond to inevitabilities, given the nature of the human organism and of the human situation?...While the specific manifestations of human nature vary between cultures...human nature is universal. All value systems have to make...concessions to [it]."[21]

As implied by the preceding comments, the anthropologists who make these claims refer to limited lists of universally accepted norms. But sometimes they seem tempted by the sweeping idea that all ultimate norms of all societies are alike. Thus, they move from the weak to the strong version of ethical universalism. Ralph Linton, for instance, speaks cautiously about "basic similarities as well as differences" among values of various societies.[22] But he also asserts: "As the social scientist's acquaintance with a large number of cultures improves, he cannot fail to be more impressed with their similarities than with their differences." This arouses the hope for empirical discovery of "a universal ethical system."[23] Clyde Kluckhohn also shifts from a limited notion of "some goals...salient for mankind in general" to a belief that both "within and between cultures moral behavior...must be judged... *with reference to principles which are not relative*."[24]

To be sure, the claim that all (or nearly all) of us in all societies share all ultimate moral views, at first glance appears clearly false. For its rebuttal, it seems enough to look around and to realize how much "people's evaluations...differ from place to place and from time to time."[25] However, according to the view under discussion, many or (in its strong version) all moral disagreements are illusory; they can be reduced to different perceptions of facts.

As indicated earlier, most nonultimate moral norms each of us accepts are inferred from a conjunction of an ultimate (or just higher level) norm and a statement of fact.[26] Many or (in the strong version) all ultimate norms of all societies are the same, as the argument goes. However, statements of fact serving as small premises for normative deductions differ from society to society (and, for that matter, even from person to person in the same society). This difference accounts for the divergence in conclusions, that is, in the norms inferred.

In this sense, conflicting factual views are claimed to be responsible for moral disagreements. But why are the factual views serving as premises for moral deductions ever in conflict? Ethical universalists point to two reasons. First, we are often prey to conflicting factual beliefs because of lack of well-established knowledge. And, second, identical discrete acts may perform entirely different functions in different social contexts. Consequently, the same discrete act can, in society X, run against one of its ultimate moral norms, but be in accord with an identical ultimate norm of society Y. Advocates of this stand provide us with instances they view as corroborating evidence.

Instances of moral conflicts due to lack of well-established knowledge abound. For example, witches were put to death in large numbers in central Europe since the mid-fifteenth century. This practice was justified by reference to facts. First, such was believed to have been the divine order: "Thou shalt not suffer a witch to live."[27] Second, witchcraft was considered a source of social disasters. Third, the stake was perceived as the way to spare the witch herself everlasting suffering in hell. More recently, Iranian zealots have been convinced that Allah orders them to kill Iraqis (and that the war dead go directly to heaven). Some churches prohibit contraception in the conviction that God embedded sex in human nature only for reproduction. The Nazis killed Jews and, less systematically, Gypsies, and various Slavic nationalities, in the belief of the racial inferiority of the victims, their intrinsic wickedness, and their innate hatred of Germany.

The moral obligation of witch killing was derived from such higher level or ultimate norms as: obey God's orders, protect your group from disasters, provide for anyone's salvation. Had a modern rationalist convinced the witch killers that there were no witches (and no divine orders to kill them, no harm done by them, no eternal suffering awaiting them), this newly acquired knowledge might have removed the moral imperative "kill the witches." The same would hold true had the Iranians been persuaded of the lack of a divine order to kill Iraqis. If the sociobiologists of today could persuade churchmen that, due to natural selection, the human sexual drive works not only for reproduction, but also as an implement of bonding, the churchmen might stop condemning the "unnatural" quality of contraception.[28] And had the Nazis been persuaded that a Jew, a Gypsy, or a Russian is not wicked and not born inferior to or hateful of Germans (and that Jewish or Gypsy parents suffer as much as German parents would, had their children been led to gas chambers), the new knowledge might have removed the moral imperative of killing.[29] In this sense, the ethical universalists blame lack of factual knowledge (on the part of those contestants who stick to false views) for the emergence of many moral conflicts. Thus, many moral conflicts are illusory; they can be reduced to factual disagreements.

Many other moral conflicts are, according to the view under discussion, illusory as well, but for a different reason. Owing to their variable social context, identical discrete acts can function differently; in particular, they can produce outcomes forbidden by an ultimate moral norm of one society, but approved by the identical ultimate norm of another. For instance, parricide runs, in the majority of societies, against such higher level or ultimate norms as "help your parents." However, according to past reports from some tribes, killing aged parents was done to spare them long periods of unmitigated suffering under nomadic conditions, and was perceived by the tribe as the child's duty of mercy, fitting the requirement "help your parents."[30]

Of course, there are differences between these two kinds of moral conflicts—conflicts ensuing from lack of knowledge, and those generated by variable social contexts of the acts under evaluation; in particular, those latter do not result from anyone's false beliefs.[31] Nonetheless, conflicts of both kinds are, so the argument goes, due to different perceptions of facts. And, reducing them to different perceptions of facts makes them illusory moral disagreements, or, more precisely, illusory *as* moral disagreements.

It is not surprising that psychologists have had their hand in developing the universalist perspective. In particular, the gestaltists reacted forcefully against the radical relativism and, especially, its psychological foundations provided by the early version of behaviorism.[32] With their holistic apprehension of cognitive fields, the gestaltists examine ethical evaluations of any act within the act's social context. This examination shows, in their view, that ethical disagreements arise out of (genuine or imagined) factual differences rather than from "diversity in ethical principles."[33] Some of the gestaltists draw a "limited conclusion from the available evidence" and maintain that "the range of cultural relativism is substantially narrowed when one takes the situational context into account."[34] Others come closer to the strong version of ethical universalism: "individuals and cultures do, on the whole, not differ widely with respect to what are considererd the ultimate ethical goals."[35] But all of them assert that if "we take into account the structural properties of experience and action, we can understand...observed differences...without abandoning the concept of human nature."[36]

The question whether the strong or the weak version is true also puzzles those human sociobiologists who favor the universalist perspective. Edward O. Wilson is most prominent among them, and I will therefore focus on his views. Some of his comments imply the strong version preference. (To be sure, in his earlier work he sounds as if he had rejected ethical universalism altogether: due to divergent human survival strategies, "no single set of moral standards can be applied to all human populations."[37] However, this contention is ambiguous enough to be disregarded in the present analysis.[38] A few years later Wilson appeared to have accepted the universalist perspective.) Building on recent developments in evolutionary biology, and reducing all life, mind, and behavior to molecular processes, Wilson claims the impending discovery of "what is humankind, what created us, and what is our purpose in the world,"[39] that is, of the ultimate meaning of life and of the human condition.[40] By answering these questions, and especially by dissecting "the machinery of the mind and [retracing] its evolutionary history,"[41] we will be able to find out how human values emerged in the course of natural selection, and, furthermore, how so many of them have outlived their original adaptive role, and became disfunctional relics, or even "hypertrophies," in the course of cultural development.[42] With this knowledge at hand, "the search for a new morality based upon a more truthful definition of man" will be possible.[43] In other words, the new, full understanding of who we are, how our mind works, and how our ethical values emerged in the process of genetic and cultural "coevolution," will provide us with the shared body of factual knowledge eliminating moral disagreements.

How will this elimination occur? On this Wilson is not always clear, but many instances scattered throughout his work provide grounds for an answer. One of the instances—the new knowledge about sex and bonding as a way of resolving disagreements over birth control—was mentioned earlier. Another instance deals with the conflict between the moralities of tribalism and humanism; to remove the conflict, it may be enough to resort to the already accumulated (even though not widely known) sociobiological information. Our genetically inherited disposition to kin altruism hypertrophied into large-scale tribalism, nationalism, and racism.[44] The hypertrophy generates frequent belief in the innate inferiority or wickedness of other tribes, nations, and races, and an ensuing feeling of hostility. But this belief is indefensible in the light of genetics. The genetic endowment of any human individual is made up of contributions by ancestors from an endless variety of ethnic groups. For instance, "the gene pool from which one modern Briton has emerged spreads over Europe, to North Africa, the Middle East, and beyond." Thus, every "individual is an evanescent combination of genes drawn from this pool, one whose hereditary material will soon be dissolved back into it."[45] Once this simple truth is understood, it easily persuades us to get rid of tribal values, to "envision the history and future of our own genes against the background of the entire human species,"[46] and then to accept the humanist ethical principles of equality and unity of the whole of human race. Wilson's belief in the feasibility of this persuasion implies an acceptance, by both parties to the conflict, of a shared higher level norm, such as: Treat your brothers (or your kin, or those like you) benevolently. The newly shared knowledge that all human beings are, from the genetic perspective, "brothers" (or kin, or basically alike), apparently constitutes the factual premise for the normative conclusion.

"Had dinosaurs grasped [this idea] they might have survived," continues Wilson, turning to another argument. "They might have been us."[47] In other words, if a species preserves its unity, the unity increases its survival fitness. This general truth—to supplement Wilson's reasoning— has not yet removed the moral conflict between tribalism and humanism, because survival of the human species was never truly at stake in known human history. Only in recent decades, due to emergence of nuclear weapons and other ecological threats of our day, the extinction of human life has become, for the first time in registered history, a distinct possibility. Wilson's just quoted words on dinosaurs seem to imply that replacing the morality of tribalism by that of humanism may now be the only way to implement the undisputed ultimate value of human survival. As soon as all of us come to understand this truth, the replacement will occur, and the moral conflict disappear.

These are just two of Wilson's instances. Others are applied to show how accumulation of knowledge can remove moral disagreements over such issues as homosexual behavior, equality of women, slavery and liberty.[48] Eventually, science may "be in a position to investigate the very origin and meaning of human values from which all ethical pronouncements...flow."[49] This "will make possible the selection of a

more deeply understood and enduring code of moral values"[50] that anyone with understanding could hardly reject. Thus, Wilson seems to have
come to prefer the strong version of ethical universalism.[51]

The same holds true of universalist moral philosophers. They join
Wilson, Linton, Kluckhohn, and others, in the preference for the strong
over the weak version, even though they also sometimes vacillate between the two. For example, Richard Brandt admits the possibility of
"*some* cases of conflicting ethical principles," but they refer to relatively unimportant problems, whereas there is "widespread agreement
on the items we care most about. Furthermore...with better understanding of the facts, the scope of agreement would be much wider."[52]
William Frankena's words also display the uncertainty of those inclined
to accept the strong version. To rebut this version,

> [o]ne must...prove that people's basic ethical and value judgments would differ
> and conflict even if they were fully enlightened and shared all the same factual
> beliefs.... To show this, one would have to find clear cases in which...these
> conditions are fulfilled and people still differ. Cultural anthropologists do not show
> us such cases; in all of their cases, there are differences in conceptual understand-
> ing and factual belief. Even when one takes two people in the same culture, one
> cannot be sure that all of the necessary conditions are fulfilled. I conclude, there-
> fore, that...relativism has not been proved and, hence, that we need not, in our
> ethical and value judgments, give up the claim that they are objectively valid in the
> sense that they will be sustained by a review by all those who are free, clear-headed,
> fully informed.[53]

The Refutation

The importance of the universalist perspective for this analysis is
clear. If true, ethical universalism provides the justification we are looking for. The justification does not consist in the sheer fact of a norm's
universal approval; a widely approved norm may be wrong, nonetheless. The justification comes from what the universal approval is claimed
to indicate. The approval constitutes, in the view under discussion, an
empirical indicator of the norm being rooted in human nature.

But is ethical universalism true? Can any of its versions be corrobo-
rated? For the answer, I will start with the strong, and then turn to the
weak version.

In the light of the preceding comments, it should be clear that the
strong version consists of two simple points. First, according to the best
available knowledge, there are no disagreements about ultimate ethical

norms, but only about norms deduced from a conjunction of ultimate (or higher level) norms and statements of fact. And, second, all these disagreements can be reduced to different perceptions of fact.

For rebuttal, it is enough to show that disagreements about ultimate ethical norms occur. Showing the disagreements is easy. For instance, there is a basic conflict between the ethical views of hedonists and perfectionists; we should pursue sensual pleasure as the only thing worthwhile, claimed Aristippus of Cyrene, whereas, for Aristotle, the development of human excellence is the ultimate ethical good. And there is a basic conflict betwen the Nietzscheans and the egalitarians; only the strong should be free and have rights, insisted Nietzsche (and Callicles), while in the words of the French Declaration, all men are free and equal in rights. Utilitarians treat punishing wrongdoers as a measure to reduce suffering, but retributivists consider punishment (even if it is ineffective in deterring crime) an ultimate demand of justice; Bentham and Beccaria recommend punishment only to prevent wrongdoing, but for Kant, even if a society resolved to dissolve itself, the last murderer in prison ought to be executed. Also the Kantian imperative never to lie, whatever the outcome of telling the truth (as exemplified by the murderer at the door dilemma), runs against the basics of utilitarian ethics.

To be sure, proponents of the strong version would perceive this refutation as begging the question. They would assert that, like all moral disagreements, these conflicts are not ultimate, but reducible to differing perceptions of facts; and the differing perceptions are due, in particular, to lack of a well-established and shared knowledge. Had these or any other ethical opponents known everything about everything feasibly relevant to their conflicting stands, the conflicts would disappear. For instance, perhaps, because of some hidden social or biological forces, all egalitarian societies are doomed to physical extinction. Or perhaps, because of our still largely unexplored genetic makeup, a rejection of liberty endangers the survival of those who reject it. Or, perhaps, the development of human excellence offends a supernatural force and thus leads to destruction of the perfectionists and their kin. Had the egalitarians or opponents of liberty or perfectionists only known of this, they would easily accept the views of their opponents.

Perhaps they would. However, knowing everything about everything feasibly relevant, accessible only to "archangels" from a celebrated metaphor by R. M. Hare,[54] is an impossible falsifier of any assertion.

That is why the strong version of ethical universalism can always be claimed to be true with impunity; one can always assert that there are some unknown, even undiscoverable relevant facts. Accordingly, the strong version resembles an article of faith rather than a testable proposition. As its major philosophical supporter admits, the ultimate ethical consensus based upon full and shared knowledge can be claimed merely "in the end...which never comes or comes only on the Day of Judgment."[55] Thus, it would be difficult to accept the universalist rejoinder.

The rejection of this rejoinder does not preclude the validity of the weak version of ethical universalism. There may still be some universally accepted ethical norms, and human rights norms may be among them. Many claimed universals have been listed earlier.[56] In the view of the universalists, these universals corroborate at least the weak version of the doctrine. However, this corroboration is, again, flawed.

The claimed universals constitute, as we have seen, a variety of norms. With respect to one group of these norms, the claim of universality is patently false. Rights and obligations arising from property and contracts do not pervade all societies; the former are tied to private property economies, the latter to market economies. And in no society, whatever its economic system, can we find the universally accepted duty of overall reciprocity in human relations.

Another group of claimed universals consists of the norms pronouncing benevolence; they express in various ways the "love your neighbor" idea. There are here prohibitions of killing and maiming, and prescriptions of kindness, sympathy, and respect for others and their rights. However, the meaning of these norms depends upon the question of who is "the neighbor," and the answer differs from one society to another. Had all societies included everybody in the world into the category of those to be benevolently treated, we would easily discover some universally accepted human rights norms. But this is not the case; in most societies, the category of neighbors has been limited to a band, tribe, nation, or subculture. Accordingly, in the event of strife, killing and maiming outsiders is not only allowed, but meritorious, and there is no duty of kindness, sympathy, or regard for them. Thus, even if there are some universally accepted norms of benevolence, they do not prescribe universal benevolence and, consequently, cannot be perceived as human rights norms.

What about the other universals listed? Some of them are simply vague enough to be acceptable in many or even all societies. There are here the norms demanding justice or fair dealing; what is perceived "just" or "fair" differs, sometimes dramatically, from one society to another,[57] and once we specify the meaning of these universally appealing terms, the universality of the norms disappears. The same holds true of such virtues as bravery; what is perceived as bravery or cowardice in some societies amounts, respectively, to foolhardiness or prudence in others.[58]

The only remaining items are the inhibition of incest and the parental commitment to protect the child. When specified, both are nearly universal.[59] The former is shared with nonhuman primate species, the latter with many lower animals as well. However, incest aversion has hardly anything to do with the human rights experience. Consequently, the prohibition of inbreeding, being clearly out of the list of human rights norms, is irrelevant for these considerations. On the other hand, the child's right to parental protection may be perceived as a nearly universal human rights experience. But it constitutes only a miniscule part of the human rights area.

Thus, not only the strong, but also the weak version of ethical universalism must be rejected.[60] If we disregard the two issues just referred to, one irrelevant, and the other one dealing with only a scintilla of the area at hand, the conclusion is clear: there is no human nature consisting in universal ethical inclinations. Accordingly (and, for some of us, distressingly), human nature thus understood cannot provide the justification we are looking for.

The Function of Ethics

As indicated earlier, there is, beyond univeral needs and wants and beyond basic ethical inclinations, also a third meaning in which human nature has been used for justification of ethics: owing to peculiarities of human nature, morality is with (or in) us to perform a specific function, and this compels us to accept the moral norms that serve the function well. Thus, the function of ethics becomes a normmaking fact claimed to justify moral norms and, among them, human rights norms.

From Social Philosophy to Social Science

The belief that morality performs a specific social function has old roots. Some moral philosophers trace it to Plato and Hobbes.[61] Plato's

Protagoras claimed that Zeus gave men moral (and legal) sense to enable them to live harmoniously together and, in this manner, to survive among wild beasts. Hobbes replaced the divine will by human teleology. He ascribed beastly characteristics to human nature; to end the war of all against all, men introduced, in the social contract, moral norms (and legal norms and sanctions). In today's thought, a group of British analytical philosophers pursue a similar path. In particular, G. J. Warnock refers explicitly to Hobbes when claiming that "the human predicament is inherently such that things are liable to go badly."[62] Owing largely to our limited sympathies, we care more about our own wants and needs than those of others. We are not only selfish, but we also display hostlity and inflict suffering on others in both individual and group encounters.[63] This is where morality comes in. "The paradigmatic moral virtues [are] those good dispositions whose tendency is directly to countervail the limitation of human sympathies."[64] Thus, "[m]orality has a practical end in view [and this is] the amelioration of human predicament,"[65] that is, elimination of suffering and increase of welfare.[66] In Toulmin's view also, the function of ethics is to harmonize "our feelings and behaviour in such a way as to make the fulfilment of everyone's aims and desires as far as possible compatible," and thus to minimize suffering and maximize welfare.[67] This "function…determines the attitude which it is 'right' for us to take,"[68] and thus provides "a good reason" for moral judgments.[69]

These views are not entirely clear. Sometimes they sound as if the function of ethics meant purpose of ethics.[70] But this implies someone's purpose, and there is no one to replace Protagoras' Zeus or the hypothetical parties to the Hobbesian contract in Warnock's or Toulmin's scheme. Sometimes, the function of ethics seems to denote an adaptive mechanism that is just there, without anyone's prior design.[71] But then the question arises how to explain the emergence of the mechanism, and, without the answer, the mechanism looks like a miracle. And, from time to time, Warnock, Toulmin, and others who display similar views, slip into tautology: they accept under the guise of functionalism, an axiological definition of morality and then derive moral norms from the definition.[72] Thus, the philosophers' attempt to justify moral norms by function of ethics is flawed.

Another, modern attempt comes from different quarters. Beholden to both system models analysis and Darwinian thought, and mediated largely through the work of Durkheim and Spencer, this attempt be-

came a major influence in sociology and social anthropology. Its proponents treat human collectivities, by analogy with living organisms, as if
the collectivities were operating systems. Ethics constitutes, in this view,
a vital component of any social system; it serves the society's adaptation. Members of any society transmit moral evaluations to one another
by routinely communicating what behavior is right and wrong, what
one should and should not do. In this manner they "turn the group into
an enormous laboratory of evaluations within which social experience
is utilized...[In this laboratory] individual evaluations undergo a process similar to the struggle for existence and natural selection: those
which are not favorable for the group are eliminated, and only
evaluations...which serve the group...remain."[73] Accordingly, negative evaluations spread in response to behavior harmful to the group,
and positive evaluations in response to useful behavior. Usually, this
process goes on without the group members being aware of its functional character; they do not know that their evaluations spread because
of the sometimes very remote social consequences of the behavior they
are evaluating. Thus, this process constitutes a basically unconscious
feedback: moral experiences and norms, even though they may originally emerge in human minds quite randomly, eventually win over the
social group and persist because of their positive outcome. In this sense,
their positive outcome is the cause of their winning and persisting. To
put it bluntly, morality is there because of its adaptive function. Which
easily brings an attempt at justification: if morality is there because of
its adaptive function, we should accept those moral norms that do serve
adaptation of the group.

The Question of Precision

At first glance, the rule of recognition just articulated seems impre-
cise; this brings the logic of the proposed justification in question. Serving adaptation of the group by morality is an ambiguous normmaking
fact: first, it is unclear which social unit constitutes "the group," and,
second, what does the "adaptation" of the group mean.

The functionalists are split on both issues. When speaking about the
group, most of them have in mind a clan, tribe, or nation; some of them
a subculture, an interest group, or social class; others a number of tribes
or states linked by such forces as religion or history; and still others

(thinking about human future rather than the past or present) the whole of the human species.[74] The "adaptation" of the group is ambivalent as well. Many functional theorists, concerned with functional explanation of the whole of culture, not only of ethics, understand the adaptation so broadly that their explanation becomes meaningless: they are always able to find a vaguely defined adaptive need served by any cultural pattern, and some of them claim, tautologically, that the very persistence of any pattern proves that an adaptive need is served by it.[75] Fortunately, functional explanation of ethics can be articulated more precisely. To be sure, moral functionalists speak about adaptation of the group in a number of different meanings, but at least each of these meanings is reasonably specific.

Sometimes, adaptation of the group means successful struggle against hostile outside forces: morality provides a tribe or nation with motivation and cohesion strong enough to effectively compete against surrounding tribes, nations, or wild animals, and either to dominate or destroy them, or at least to survive among them.[76] In a closely related view, morality, as a particularly efficient motivation for cooperative behavior, constitutes a factor contributing to, or even a necessary condition for the very existence of any society, or, at least, of any stable, orderly society—a "glue" that, along with other motivations, binds individuals into a harmoniously operating social system.[77] In the view of those who treat the whole of the human species as one all-embracing group, adaptation of the group easily amounts to the state of universal human brotherhood, benevolence, equality.[78] For still others, the adaptation of the group is to be reduced to the welfare of its individual members,[79] and that reduction lays ground for acceptance of some version of utilitarianism as a primary moral system.[80] Thus, because of the ambiguity of "the function," the meaning of the functional justification varies. However, in none of its variations is this a hopelessly vague meaning. As we will see later, the various meanings just specified (that is, the occurrence of the various claimed normmaking facts) are precise enough to make the proposition testable.[81]

But, even though its meaning has been sharpened, there still is a problem with the logic of the functional justification: the very idea of morality being with us as an adaptive tool is enigmatic. It sounds as mysterious as some of the philosophical assertions noted earlier. In a living organism, the adaptive emergence of various organs is reasonably clear in the light of natural selection.[82] But how can anyone explain, short of a miracle, an analogous role of moral evaluations in human society?

Of course, one could try to find an explanation at the individual level by stressing the cognitive process: aware of the dependence of each of us on the society we live in, we decide to accept the socially useful and to reject socially harmful moral norms. However, this would amount to conscious teleology which the functionalists reject; their "teleology" is explicitly unintentional, "unconsciously brilliant" in the words of Petrażycki.[83]

But where could this unconscious and unintentional "teleology" possibly come from? Short of referring to the supernatural, there seems to be no answer to this question, unless the adaptive outcomes of moral experiences can be ascribed to some force, hidden within human nature, which, by generating those experiences, drives us, without our knowledge, into behavior useful for the group. This kind of explanation does not imply a purpose conceived by human intellect; it implies adaptive operation on the part of a force concealed within each of us. But where would such a force reside? Would it be located in a specific part of our body, or in our mind (if mind is not reducible to body)? And how could it be detected and scrutinized? Darwin himself speculated vaguely about "our moral sense...originating in the *social instincts*" and resulting in the group selection process, by making a morally advanced tribe "victorious over most other tribes."[84] But this speculation did not answer any of these questions. And the functionally oriented sociologists and anthropologists did not even try to provide an answer.

From Social Science to Sociobiology

Then, rather unexpectedly, a kind of answer was offered in recent decades. Since the 1960s, a number of modern evolutionary biologists—molecular biologists and sociobiologists—have been claiming the discovery of a force, hidden within us, that generates ethics as an adaptive mechanism; the force is encoded in the human genetic program. This claim is beholden to a number of antecedent scholarly developments, all of them rooted in neo-Darwinian evolutionary theory.[85]

The views of biologists who ascribe the adaptive function of moral experience to the operation of genes vary. Despite this variation, however, there is a common core to their views. The majority of them are materialists and philosophical reductionists: they treat the evolution of species as a part of cosmic evolution, and they reduce all forms of life, from bacteria to homo sapiens, to physicochemical processes at the molecular level; this reduction encompasses all characteristics of organisms. Having accepted this sweeping perspective, they claim to have resolved (or, at least, they promise to resolve) the most fundamental of mysteries: the origin and evolution of the universe, the origin and evolution of life, the emergence of animal and human consciousness and of human self-consciousness. And, as I noted in a different context in the preceding chapter, they announce a new perception of the ultimate meaning of life and of the human condition: we are quickly discovering "what is humankind, what created us, and what is our purpose in the world."[86]

The origin of the universe is traced back to the big bang[87] "Life and mind have a physical basis."[88] Life is hypothesized to have emerged as an outcome of a coincidental (and, possibly, unique) event—an "essentially unpredictable" case of synthesis of inanimate matter.[89] Phylogenetic characteristics of any species are outcomes of natural selection, and there are among them animal and human consciousness and human self-consciousness and thought. Consciousness, self-consciousness and thought are claimed to be only the genetically programmed epiphenomena of the brain;[90] this claim amounts to physiological resolution of the body-mind problem.

Natural selection plays an obviously crucial role in this perception of life. However, its Darwinian meaning has been specified here in a new manner. Studies of self-sacrificial altruism undermined the belief that evolutionary struggle is conducted by organisms just for their own survival; when the herd is under attack, various species, from termites to injury mimicking birds, sacrifice their organisms for the survival of others. That is why the idea of individual selection has been replaced by the "inclusive fitness" hypothesis: the genetic code of any individual organism is programmed to produce characteristics, among them behavior, maximizing reproduction of the organism's own genotype within the population. Of course, any organism's genotype is, to a varying degree, replicated in its offspring and nondescendant relatives; thus, all of them constitute "a potential avenue of genetic reproduction."[91] This notion of natural selection explains the organism's self-sacrifice not only for its offspring, but also for other kin; according to Hamilton's well-known formula, the self-sacrifice makes genetic sense, and thus tends to occur, whenever it brings about positive balance in the organism's self-replication.

Thus, in the view under discussion, natural selection means the gene-selection process. And, since all living species have emerged in its course, the recognition of this process provides us with understanding of the true and ultimate meaning of all life. Any living organism is "merly a transition, a stage between what was and what will be.... It strives to prepare an identical programme for the following generation[s]... [thus,] reproduction [of its genetic material] represents both the beginning and the end, the cause and the aim."[92] In other words, "the individual organism is only...part of an elaborate device to preserve and spread" its genes.[93] Of course, so is the human organism: all our phylogenetic characteristics are outcomes of natural selection serving survival and replication of the genotype of each of us.

Our "phylogenetic characteristics" are understood here in a broad, panselectionist manner. They include, basically, not only our anatomy and physiology, but also our mind and its products, and our social behavior. Thus, our thought, emotional propensities, and social behavior, even though diversified (in response to variable cultural and ecological pressures) have emerged as genetically programmed implements of our inclusive fitness. All of them carry out the commands of genes—they are the genes' "techniques for replicating themselves."[94]

Morality is, from this perspective, just one such technique. It is claimed that the human ability to ontogenetically develop the specifically human moral experiences emerged as a mutation over five million years ago, among hunters-gatherers living in small, endogamously breeding kinship bands.[95] By providing a strong altruistic and cooperative motivation, this ability enhanced the inclusive fitness of the carriers of the "moral gene." Consequently, the ability became, in the process of selection, an increasingly universal characteristic of the human species.[96] This clarifies not only the origin, but also the function of ethics: moral experiences, generated by the human genetic program, promote "the survival and multiplication of the genes" of their carriers;[97] thus the experiences help the DNA of their carriers to survive and spread within the population (and, in this manner, they helped, millions years ago, the popultion itself—that is, the human species—to survive among animal predators). Accordingly, in Wilson's sweeping words, "human behavior—like the deepest capacities which drive and guide it—is the circuitous technique by which human genetic material has been and will be kept intact. Morality has no other demonstrable ultimate function."[98] And this provides the more specific explanation we have been looking for: our genetic program—segments of DNA molecules located at a specific chromosome position—is the hidden force which generates the adaptive phenomenon of moral experience.

The Genetic Explanation Examined

Whether this genetic explanation of the "teleology" of moral experience is true is an open question, and I will return to it soon. But, if true, this explanation brings about an unforseen conclusion. We turned to the explanation to further clarify the mystery of the adaptive role of morality, and thus to enhance the logic of its functional justification. However, unexpectedly, the explanation rebuts the functional justification instead of supporting it.

The functional justification rests on the acceptance of the normmaking fact: morality is there because it helps the society (or the social group, or men in society) to adjust. However, if the genetic explanation is true, the assertion of this normmaking fact becomes false; the explanation, by stressing gene selection and not group adjustment, finds the function of morality not in the society's enhanced adaptive capacity, but in the individual's enhanced capacity to preserve and replicate his or her genetic material. Thus, if the genetic explanation of morality is true, it may be claimed to justify only the ultimate value of self-replication; that is, everyone's duty to promote maximum replication of his or her own genotype.[99]

How persuasive is this value? Its appeal seems nil. Even though the majority of us do care about the survival of our children and grandchildren, because we "know and love them, [we] may have no regard for more remote descendants" of ours or our collateral relatives.[100] And, indeed, it seems that it would be difficult to find anyone truly concerned about the very distant future of his or her genotype; who would ever care about his or her DNA multiplying through thousands or millions of years? This means that the norm prescribing one's maximum replication within the long-lived human genetic pool is quite irrelevant for our moral concerns; it sounds nearly as irrelevant as the prescription that we clasp hands three times an hour. By being irrelevant, this norm becomes unpersuasive. And thus, with the circularity indicated earlier,[101] its rule of recognition loses its compelling force as well.[102] Which, of course, amounts to the rebuttal of this norm's functional justification. No wonder proponents of the genetic explanation never use this explanation to justify their moral views.[103]

The genetic explanation implies more than that, however. If true, it precludes not only the validity of the functional justification, but also of all other traditionally claimed justifications. Within the view of the world and of ethics accepted by proponents of this explanation, there is no room for such normmaking facts as divine will, intuitionist ontology, existence of pure reason as the source of ethics, or of human nature understood otherwise than as a genetic fitness implement. That is why no proponent of the genetic explanation supports any kind of objective justification of morality;[104] they understand that, once their explanation is considered true, all justifications fail.

This brings us to the basic question: is the genetic explanation true? The question cannot be answered in a publicly convincing way. It may well be true; it is possible that whatever exists is matter, that life can be reduced to physicochemical processes and mind to physiology, and that human morality is there since it promotes replication of the carriers of the "moral gene." But any of these claims can be false as well; none of them has been tested, and some, if not all of them, are untestable. Thus, the agnostics may be right when claiming that we will never be able to resolve the mysteries under discussion. In particular, "we may be faced with the possibility that the origin of life (like the origin of the universe) becomes an impenetrable barrier to science...[Also] the problem of the emergence of consciousness...[and the] body mind problem" can be insoluble.[105] And, most importantly, the panselectionist stand and, especially, the belief "that human values are determined or fixed genetically...is doubtful to say the least,"[106] and, possibly, untestable.[107] Thus, we are not, and may never be, able to determine whether the genetic explanation of ethics is true. This indeterminacy is most relevant for our analysis; unproved and uncertain, the genetic explanation cannot be used for rebuttal of the functional justification (and other justifications) of morality. Consequently, the functionalists may reject the genetic explanation and still claim that new discoveries should detect and correctly specify the force—let's call it "social instincts" or otherwise—embedded in us and responsible for the adaptive functioning of ethics. The claim, however, leaves them with the mystery of "teleology," again, unresolved. This amounts to a major flaw in their logic. But perhaps the flaw is not fatal, and thus does not amount to definitive rebuttal of the functional justification. Like many other vague theoretical constructs in various areas of scientific knowledge, the unspecified "instinctive" force, embedded in us and responsible for the adaptive operation of morality, may be believed to be detectable and to be made clear in the future.

The Refutation

As indicated earlier, any claimed justification of morality can be feasibly rebutted on any one of three grounds: defect of logic, lack of persuasive force, or the evidence that the claimed normmaking fact has not occurred. I have been trying to rebut the functional justification on the first two grounds, and the attempt was not entirely effective. Now I will turn to the third of them. This means answering a factual question: is it true that moral evaluations eventually win over the social group and persist if, and only if, they serve adaptation of the group?

This ambiguous question was clarified in the preceding comments; various meanings of the "group" and "adaptation" have been, to a degree, sharpened. With its precision enhanced, the normmaking fact—the adaptive function of ethics—is at least specific enough for its occurrence to be empirically assessed; well-known data from human history can be used as potential falsifiers of the functional justification.

By this I mean data from human history, not prehistory. To be sure, sociobiologists perceive prehistory as an era when morality served group adaptation. As mentioned earlier, they hypothesize that during the five million years preceding registered history, morality, as a gene selection implement, was enhancing the survival ability of human kinship groups. And, since the kinship group was identical with the social group (that is, with "the society" of that time), this process meant group selection. In this sense, the good of the social group can be claimed to have been the function of morality in the era preceding the advent of history.

This hypothesis may seem viable if morality is understood as instinctive, animal-like altruism, similar to that of termites or bees. However, with the less arbitrary, more "human" meaning of morality implied in this discussion, the hypothesis could hardly be accepted. As noted earlier, morality is understood here as both a peculiar kind of experiences, especially right-duty experiences, and as evaluative judgments expressing those experiences. It is clear that, with this understanding of morality, the belief in its group-selectionist role five million years ago can hardly be assumed and cannot feasibly be tested. Indeed, morality might have been totally absent at that and much later time. Owing to the level of cognitive capacity of our distant ancestors, it is plausible that ethics—the feelings of right, duty, guilt or shame, as well as their linguistic expressions—was unknown among them; the more so that the emergence of these feelings in any population may depend upon the population's mental ability to verbally express them.[108] That is why only data from registered human history can be used to test the functional justification.

And those data abound. There is no doubt that, in the course of human history, innumerable moral evaluations which won over various societies, have served the adjustment of the group, in one or another of the meanings of "adjustment" and "the group" accepted here; the list ranges from the Ten Commandments for the Hebrews, to the work ethic for various European and Europe-derived nations, norms proclaiming the rights of man for America since the eve of the American Revolution, and the majority of moral prohibitions sanctioned by criminal codes of many states, such as prohibition of murder, battery, theft, arson. However, there is also no doubt that innumerable maladaptive moral evaluations have won the majority of human minds in various societies. Their long list includes the evaluations underlying the Inquisition, religious wars of the past and present,[109] the anarchist liberties preceding partitions of Poland; it also includes the ethical components of Nazi ideology. The last item (even though shorter-lived than the others) is a startling case. The Nazi moral directives largely won the minds of the Germans in the1930s, and the outcome proved to be maladaptive, whichever of the just stipulated meanings of "adaptation" and "group" we accept. It became a disaster for the German nation and all subcultures, interest groups, and territorial units within Germany. It became a disaster for the whole of Europe and for a substantial part of the human species. And, if the good of the group is reduced to the welfare of its individual members, Nazi morality brought about suffering and loss of life of unprecedented proportion within all the involved populations—from the Holocaust, to torturing and partially destroying various occupied nations of Europe, to over thirty milion war-dead in the Western hemisphere, among them over four million Germans. Thus, not only have maladaptive evaluations won over various societies, but, moreover, the magnitude of their harmful effects has been striking.

This magnitude can be easily explained; it is due to the stimulating force of moral experiences. As I noted earlier, moral experiences have energizing properties. They drive those who feel duty bound to fulfill the obligations, and they drive those experiencing their rights (or experiencing rights of others) to pursue the claims. They provide a reliable and inexpensive motivation.[110] And they become truly powerful whenever counteracted or provoked.

The force of the counteracted or provoked moral experiences rises irrespective of their contents. Accordingly, counteraction and provocation can stimulate feelings of the right and duty to fight for human well-being, dignity, or equal treatment. But counteraction and provocation (such as the Reichstag fire or Kirov's assassination) can also stimulate the feelings of the right and duty to humiliate, enslave, and destroy others, especially in the name of a fanatical ideology or blind loyalty to a leader, party, tribe. This means that the moral motivation can spread, win and operate with great force in the name of the most adaptive or maladaptive kind of moral system (and, in evaluative language, in the name of the best or the worst kind). And, if the latter is the case, the power of the moral motivation generates disasters.[111]

Thus, the resort to historical data brings about a clear conclusion. The functional justification of ethics, having barely survived the challenge dealing with its logic, fails easily on empirical grounds. It is simply not true that whatever eventually wins in the struggle among evaluations is optimal for the group. That is, it is not true, unless "eventually" is understood as indefinitely as to feasibly refer to eternity. But were this understanding to be accepted, the final optimal outcome would become an article of faith that could never be rebutted; in any society, on every consecutive day, the optimal outcome could be claimed to be coming tomorrow, and again tomorrow, *ad infinitum*.

What is the significance of this conclusion? There are three reasonably clear meanings of "human nature" as a claimed justification of human rights norms, and all of them have been analyzed here. In its first two meanings—as universal needs and wants, and as universal ethical inclinations—human nature did not provide the justification we are looking for, and now it has failed in the third of its meanings. Thus, our search for justification must go beyond human nature.

Notes

1. This persuasive appeal is not quite universal, however. Hobbes was not persuaded, nor, in the wake of the Second World War, were "scientists and intellectuals [who] increasingly came to emphasize...their belief in human...independence from the cruel and mindless world of nature" (Kaye 1986: 39).
2. Russell 1962: 107. But Russell does not refer to nature for justification of ethical norms. As a utilitarian, he considers avoidance of suffering as the reason why universal human needs ought to be met.
3. Cf. e.g., Selznick 1961: 93.
4. Grotius 1853, vol.I, prolegomenon 6.
5. *Ibid.*, prolegomenon 19.
6. Selznick 1961: 93.
7. Selznick, *ibid.* In Locke's view (1924: 180), these needs and wants, especially the want to preserve liberty, brought "men uniting into commonwealths, and putting themselves under governments."
8. See, for example, Bay: 53–75.
9. In his many works, Abraham H. Maslow has provided the most elaborate catalog of needs and wants claimed as universal; see in particular Maslow 1959: 119-35; 1970, chapter 7; 1976, appendix D.
10. This is particularly true of Maslow and his followers. Not only does he claim that "[f]acts create oughts" (1976: 115), but he accepts the entailment of rights by basic needs firmly enough to identify the former with the latter: "it is legitimate and fruitful to regard instinctoid basic needs...as *rights* as well as needs" (1970: xiii); "the basic needs are probably common to all mankind and are therefore shared values" (1959: 122).
11. Cf. ch. 2, n. 57 and ch. 6, n. 11, *infra.*
12. And they may never be able to sway it, if critics of utilitarianism (most notably Donegan, Rescher, Rawls) are correct when they claim that utilitarianism runs against some of our most deeply embedded moral intuitions.
13. That is why John Stuart Mill's controversial "proof" of the principle of utility does not justify utilitarianism. In his words, since "human nature is so constituted as to desire nothing which is not either a part of happiness or a means to happiness, we can have no other proof, and we require no other, that these are the only things desirable" (1972: 36). Moore and others have labeled these rather opaque words as the naturalistic fallacy—a dubious criticism in the light of Mill's other assertions, especially on logic. It seems reasonable to interpret these words as an attempt at a justification of utilitarianism; according to this interpretation, the only feasible justification (or "proof") of utilitarian doctrine is the universal persuasiveness of the fact that all humans desire happiness and happiness only. Thus understood, Mill's attempted justification fails; but at least it does not suffer from the naturalistic fallacy.
14. For example, in Cicero's view, "since an intelligence common to us all makes things known to us...honourable actions are ascribed by us to virtue and dishonourable actions to vice; and only a madman would conclude that these

judgements are matters of opinion, and not fixed by nature" (1928: Book I, XIV, 45). And Grotius treated the acceptance of a principle among the nations as "proof a posteriori" that it was a norm of the law of nature (1853, Book I, Ch, I/ XII, 1).

15. For example, "The relativist point of view brings into relief the validity of every set of norms for the people whose lives are guided by them" (Herskovits 1948: 76); "The recognition of cultural relativity carries with it its own values, which need not be those of the absolutist philosophies. [It accepts] equally valid patterns of life which mankind has created for itself [as] new bases for tolerance" (Benedict 1934: 278).

16. The former assertion is not necessarily implied, since universal approval of norms does not constitute their only feasible justification. And the latter assertion is a non sequitur, because the bare factual statement that norms of different societies differ does not entail any evaluative conclusions.

17. "There is no ethical principle on which all individuals will be found in agreement," claims Linton (1952: 648). "Every society includes a sprinkling of imbeciles, psychotics, and actively anti-social persons.... When we say that a society has a particular ethical system, we mean that a large majority of its members accept this system."

18. Linton 1952: 651–59; 1954: 466, 470; Kluckhohn 1955: 671–72. See also Redfield 1962: 440.

19. Duncker 1939: 51; Asch 1952: 378.

20. Brandt 1959: 95.

21. Kluckhohn 1955: 676.

22. Linton 1954: 461.

23. Linton 1952: 647.

24. Kluckhohn 1955: 674, 676.

25. Stevenson 1963: 77.

26. See 19–20, *supra.*

27. Exodus XXII, 18. The impact of this norm has been stressed particularly strongly by Bertrand Russell (1962: 25).

28. Wilson 1978: 146–47.

29. Of course, this new knowledge would not have removed a moral imperative of killing based on a duty of blind obedience. Nor would it have removed greed or fear of sanction or sheer sadism as motives for killing.

30. Simmons 1945: 232–41; Duncker 1939: 41–43.

31. In the latter kind of conflicts, the two opposing factual beliefs may both be true; they do not contradict each other. There is no contradiction between the statements: "in society A killing old parents helps them" and "in society B killing old parents does not help them."

32. Asch 1952: 371–75.

33. *Ibid.*, 377. See also Wertheimer 1935: 353–67.

34. Asch 1968: 166.

35. Frenkel-Brunswick 1954: 470.

36. Asch 1952: 383.

37. Wilson 1976: 363–64.

38. The contention may have at least three different meanings. First, it may preclude the universal acceptance of a single, complete system of ultimate moral norms. Second, it may preclude the universal acceptance of even a few from among such norms. And third, it may only preclude the universal acceptance of nonultimate moral norms, each of them inferred from a higher level norm and a factual premise.

In the first understanding, Wilson's contention opposes the strong version of universalism, in the second—both the strong and the weak version, and in the third it does not oppose either. That the third might have been close to Wilson's mind, is implied by the following words: for survival's sake, "the moral standards of individuals during early phases of colony growth should differ *in many details* from those of individuals at demographic equilibrium or during episodes of overpopulation. Metapopulations subject to high levels of r extinction will tend to diverge genetically from other kinds of populations in ethical behavior"(*ibid.*, emphasis added).

39. Lumsden and Edward O. Wilson 1983: 7.
40. Wilson 1980: 28.
41. Wilson 1978: 4-5, 196.
42. *Ibid.*, 89-97.
43. *Ibid.*, 4.
44. *Ibid:*, 92.
45. *Ibid.*, 197.
46. *Ibid.*
47. *Ibid.*
48. *Ibid.*, 80-81, 128-29, 134-35, 142-47, 198-99; Wilson 1976: 555; 1980: 69.
49. Wilson 1978: 5.
50. *Ibid.*, 186. See also Wilson 1980: 52, 72.
51. Wilson's views are discussed here only as an important instance of ethical universalism; if true, these views provide an empirical indicator of human nature in the sense accepted in this article. However, Wilson himself, in contrast with Kluckhohn and Asch (see 30, 32-33, *supra*), does not treat ethical universalism as an empirical indicator of human nature. Consequently, he does not treat the universal acceptance of a moral norm as justification of that norm.
52. Brandt 1959: 288 (and 102-103).
53. Frankena 1963: 93-94, 96.
54. For the final version of the metaphor see the chapter "The Archangel and the Prole," in Hare 1981: 44-64.
55. Frankena 1963: 96.
56. See 29-30, *supra*.
57. To be sure, there seems to be one universal component of justice in any society. To be perceived as just, any distribution (of good or burdens, rewards, or punishments) must be consistent; that is, it must follow the precept: Treat like cases alike, and varying cases according to relevant differences among them (as articulated by Gustav Radbruch, see 130 and ch. 6, n. 10, *infra*). However, even then, the universality is spurious. The characteristics which make the likeness of cases, and the differences among them, relevant, are variable (cf. ch. 6, n. 12, *infra*). They include in some, but not in other societies, such items as race, ethnicity, sex, wealth, caste ascription, physical fitness, intellectual ability, political loyalties, or religious affiliation.
58. This ambiguity of "bravery" has been thoughtfully analyzed by Lazari-Pawłowska 1970: 23-24.
59. They are nearly, but not entirely universal. Incest, especially brother-sister marriage, was approved among the royalty of various ancient states, and seems to have been quite widespread in Egypt (see, e.g., Hopkins 1980: 303-54). Also the full universality of parental protection may be questioned in view of the early

Roman norms of *patria potestas* or of female infanticide, especially in China and India (cf. Dickemann 1979: 321-67).

60. The rejection of ethical universalism should not disguise the merits of the doctrine. Asch, Linton, Wilson, and others, have convincingly demonstrated that a large proportion of ethical conflicts can be reduced to different perceptions of facts. This itself is a contention of major importance for our understanding of human behavior and for policy purposes. It also paves the way for better comprehension of the widely debated role of rationality in ethics.

61. Mackie 1977: 108-10.

62. Warnock 1971: 17.

63. *Ibid.*, 21-22.

64. *Ibid.*, 9.

65. *Ibid.*, 16.

66. *Ibid.*, 27-34.

67. Toulmin 1958: 137.

68. *Ibid.*, 169.

69. *Ibid.*, p. 224.

70. Cf., e.g., Warnock 1971: 15-16.

71. Cf., e.g., Toulmin 1958: 134-36, 170-71.

72. Occasionally, each of them turns the substantial question, "what is morality for?" into a semantic one, "according to the meaning of 'moral,' what is morality for?" Even in this articulation, the question sounds metaethical, as if they were asking about the object of any morality, their own or entirely alien. But it is easy to insert into this question the normative meaning of 'moral,' and this is what they sometimes do. They have been strongly influenced by utilitarian thought (even though some of them, especially Warnock, are not consequentialists). Thus, they smuggle into the 'moral' those evaluations proscribe harming others and prescribe promotion of human well-being, especially satisfaction of important wants and needs. We cannot reject these evaluations "without completely abandoning the very ideas of 'duty' and of 'ethics,'" claims Toulmin (1958: 143); this is "the way in which reasoning must be designed to influence behaviour if it is to be called 'ethical'" (1958: 131). And Warnock maintains that "not just anything can function as a criterion of *moral* evaluation.... [T]he limits are set somewhere within the general area of concern with the welfare of human beings...of course, we do not *choose* that this should be so; it *is* so simply because of what 'moral' means" (Warnock 1967: 67ff). Thus, on semantic grounds, elimination of human suffering and promotion of human welfare are what morality is for, and this is believed to justify acceptance of utilitarian norms. Of course, this reasoning is faulty. Its proponents smuggle utilitarian norms into the definition of morality, and then easily derive these norms from the definition.

73. This is Petrażycki's articulation of the view under discussion, as summarized, in 1954, by Jerzy Lande (for a more inclusive English translation, see Lande 1975: 34-35; cf. also Petrażycki 1955: 327-30). This is, basically, a Darwinian view of the ethics. "A truly Darwinian thinker would surely view the values...of a people as forming...a population which is more or less well adapted to the needs of the men concerned, and within which individual practices can change more or less independently in the face of new socio-historical situations, in a pragmatic manner, and with more or less 'adaptive' consequences" (Toulmin 1982: 152-53).

74. On the "variation in the *unit* [served] by the imputed function" see Merton 1968: 80, 106. Cf. also Durkheim 1965: 52.
75. For various instances of this stand and its incisive criticism, see Merton 1968: 84-90. Cf. also Hempel 1965: 322.
76. On the "group selectionist" model of this view, as originally articulated by Darwin, see 42, *infra*.
77. The question of what "binds" human individuals into society as an operating system has been a long-lasting concern of social scientists. Many of them (most notably Durkheim, Petrażycki, Parsons, Radcliffe-Brown) stress here morality's essential role.
78. This stand, widespread among humanist and religious philosophers, was spelled out by Darwin as an evolutionary prediction: "At all times throughout the world tribes have supplanted other tribes [in the process of natural selection]; and as morality is one important element in their success, the standard of morality... will thus everywhere tend to rise and increase.... As man advances in civilization, and small tribes are united into larger communities, the simplest reason would tell each individual that he ought to extend his social instincts and sympathies to all the members of the same nation, though personally unknown to him. This point being once reached, there is only an artificial barrier to prevent his sympathies extending to the men of all nations and races... [among them] to the imbecile, maimed, and other useless members of society" (Darwin 1896: 122, 124-25, 132). For a parallel evolutionary prediction by Petrażycki, see Lande, 1975: 34-35.
79. Bronislaw Malinowski was the main proponent of this stand. As stressed in various accounts of his field work, culture—with morality as one of its aspects—is a part of "an instrumental apparatus" which, by contributing "towards a more closely knit social texture, towards the wider and more penetrating distribution of services and goods... ideas and beliefs," contributes to satisfaction of human needs—biological, derived, and integrative" (Malinowski: 1960: 150, 170, 175).
80. Cf. the penetrating comments by Brandt 1959: 255-58.
81. Moreover, in the light of these meanings, it is clear how genuine the appeal of this justification is. In particular, it is easy for tribal zealots and nationalists to perceive the functional stand as justification of their tribalism or nationalism. It is also easy for the champions of all-human brotherhood to perceive the functional stand as justification of their beliefs, and, for the utilitarians, to perceive it as justification of utilitarianism.
82. It is, of course, only as clear as the theory of natural selection itself; for a sharp criticism of some problems with the theory (in particular, of the question of "how a complicated organ, such as the eye, can ever result from the purely accidental co-operation of independent mutations"), see Popper 1979: 241-42, 256-84; the sentence quoted appears on p. 273.
83. Petrażycki 1959-60, vol.2: 679-81. This unintentional, unconsciously useful character is also accepted by Durkheim (in particular in 1965, *passim*, and 1938: 89-97.
84. Darwin 1896: 132 (emphasis added), and chapters 4 and 5, *passim*.
85. The developments include the ethologists' emphasis on social behavior as an outcome of natural selection, the synthesis of Darwin's and Mendel's thought into population genetics, Hamilton's theorem of "inclusive fitness," and, in particular, the sucessful scrutiny of the DNA molecule and the breaking of the genetic code.
86. Lumsden and Wilson 1983: 7.

87. Wilson 1978: 202. To be sure, Wilson admits that neither Leibnitz's question of why is there something rather than nothing, nor the question where did the ultimate units of matter come from, can be answered with finality (pp. 1, 201); nonetheless, "scientific materialism [and] its evolutionary epic" are claimed to provide the best answer (p.201).
88. *Ibid.*
89. Monod 1971: 42-44, 140-46. See also Crick 1966: 66-71.
90. Cf, e.g., Wilson 1978: 2-6; Monod 1969: 14-15.
91. Alexander 1979: 45.
92. Jacob 1973: 2.
93. Wilson 1976: 3.
94. *Ibid.*, 3, 23; for a later, detailed elaboration of this view within the broad scheme of the "gene-culture coevolution," see Lumsden and Wilson 1981. Many other sociobiologists and molecular biologists accept this panselectionist stand, among them Monod, Crick, Alexander, Dawkins, and Barash.
95. Wilson 1978: 34, 153.
96. This process is claimed to parallel the emergence of animal, self-sacrificial "altruism," and its spread among various social species, most notably social insects. Cf., in particular, Wilson 1976: 3-4, 106-29, and Wilson 1978: 153.
97. Wilson 1978: 2, 5-6.
98. *Ibid.*, 167.
99. To be sure, this genetically explained function of morality might be read in a different manner: by promoting survival and proliferation of the genes of their carriers, moral experiences help the human species to survive. Thus interpreted, the genetic explanation could be feasibly claimed to justify the ultimate value of human survival. However, thus interpreted, the genetic explanation would, at least partially, contradict the views of its proponents. Even though its proponents assume that moral experiences promoted human survival in distant prehistory, none of them claims that morality performs this function any more.

   In their view, owing to his cognitive skills, historical man achieved early on an unprecedented state of ecological release by removing or neutralizing his animal competitors. The following growth of human population brought about replacement of kinship bands by newly emerging tribes and nations. The resulting competition for resources has generated a new morality of tribalism and nationalism—a hard-core, self-sacrificial altruism in favor of one's tribe or nation. This new morality is claimed to constitute, in Wilson's words, a "hypertrophy" of the "biological predisposition" (1978: 92,116). It has been producing tribal and national wars—a degree of intraspecific strife otherwise unknown in the biosphere (Monod 1971: 161; Alexander 1987: 228). Today, with modern weapons in our hands, the wars may easily spell the ultimate disaster: destruction of human life and, feasibly, of all life on earth. (On this and some other dangers for human survival see, e.g., Alexander 1987: xiii, 32-33, 193, 227-52; Barash 1982: 353-54; Monod 1971: 164ff.) That is why some proponents of this view suggest, in the name of human survival, that ethics be deliberately removed from human minds and replaced by "soft-core altruism" (or, in Robert L. Trivers's wording, "reciprocal altruism"), that is, teleological motivation of reciprocity (cf. Wilson 1978: 154-65, and, especially, his belief that the "hard-core altruism...is the enemy of civilization," p. 157). Thus, the general claim that ethics serves human survival would clearly contradict their views; they perceive destruction rather than survival of the human species as the impending outcome of morality.

100. Singer 1981: 79.
101. On 21-22, *supra*.
102. But, assuming the unfeasible, if this norm were experienced as relevant, it would hardly be persuasive anyway; it would be considered flagrantly egoistic and nepotist, and thus to run against moral intuitions of this and many other societies.
103. However, many of them use the explanation to reject various traditional, especially religious, normmaking facts, and thus to justify the rejection of the moral norms derived from those facts. In Monod's words, this means rejecting "a disgusting farrago of Judeo-Christian religiosity...[and Marxist] religion of history" (1971: 171).
104. This, of course, does not prevent them from spelling out their own, independent moral norms or moral systems (that is, moral norms and systems independent of any justification, especially religious); being unconstrained by any normmaking facts, they feel free to accept personal responsibility for whatever values each of them accepts. Thus, each of them advocates his own moral views—even those who (like Wilson) suggest replacement of ethics by teleology, and those who (like Alexander 1987: 191) believe that, basically, our moral motivation constitutes only an instrumental deception, and, whenever it happens to genuinely occur, "it represents an evolutionary mistake." For a critical review of their moral views (including various versions of utilitarianism, liberalism and socialism, benevolence and disinterested altruism in the ordinary, "human" sense, harmonious operation of societies, the ultimate value of human survival and of scientific knowledge, as well as Confucian and Taoist values), see Kaye 1986, chapters 3, 4, 5.
105. Popper 1974: 270, 273.
106. Dobzhansky 1974: 201-2.
107. In the words of another critic, by "[l]eaping from molecules to man, molecular biologists have exaggerated the degree of genetic determination of human behavior and the human mind well beyond that for which there is clear scientific warrant" (Kaye 1986: 93).
108. On this role of language, see Brandt (1979: 168-69), who refers to the seminal work of Martin L. Hoffman on the psychology of moral development.
109. Cf. Merton (1968: 83), on the disfunctional role of religious conflicts and the Inquisition.
110. Moral experiences are, in various ways, more reliable than other kinds of motivation. For instance, they are often more reliable than fear in preventing wrongdoing. This is so for several reasons. First, basically, fear of sanction prevents wrongdoing only as long as the threat is there. Second, even in the presence of the threat, the daring are more effectively prevented from wrongdoing by belief in its immorality than by fear. Moreover, fear of sanction works best as a deterrent for only one portion of wrongful behavior—commitment of calculated acts, like profesional theft or killing for hire; unpremeditated, highly emotional behavior is much less deterrable. On the other hand, internalized aversion effectively prevents both calculated and emotional wrongdoing (cf. Gorecki 1983: 70). Furthermore, the inexpensive operation of morality contributes to its effectiveness: anyone's moral motivation is self-administered and thus costs nothing, whereas systems of sanctions, especially criminal sanctions, are costly, and sometimes their costs, by being prohibitive, undermine the operation of those systems.
111. This is why some sociobiologists recommend replacement of ethics by teleology, see note ch. 2, n. 104, *supra*.

3

Beyond Human Nature

The list of feasible justifications registered earlier includes, besides human nature, three kinds of normmaking facts. The first is the fact that the norm has been stipulated by a heteronomous, authoritative "source," the second—that the norm is a necessary dictate of reason, and the third—that the norm is true. All three have a common peculiar characteristic: by transcending human nature, they presume broader assertions about the ultimate nature of the world, or about our knowledge of the world, or both.

The Divine Will

The divine will does not provide the only claimed heteronomous justification of ethics; sometimes, adherents of authority in ethics resort to "sources" of norms other than God's orders. As I noted earlier, these sources include the social contract; they also include demands of monarchs, dictators, ancestors, or tutelary spirits. It is clear, however, that most of these sources provide a justification that is persuasive only for the relatively few. For instance, the fact that a norm was uttered by a monarch or dictator may be persuasive for some of his subjects but not for others or for inhabitants of other states. Thus, even if a sovereign—a Marcus Aurelius or a Napoleon—utters a norm pronouncing universal human rights (which happens rarely; autocrats tend to stress only the rights of their tribe, if not only of their own), it does not provide a valid justification. The social contract does not provide a valid justification either. To be experienced as binding, the social contract would have to be understood as a genuine historical fact, and not as a philosophical fiction. Furthermore, this understanding would have to be accompanied by the conviction that the consensus of ancestors binds later generations. But, however powerful was the impact of the contractarian stand on the past development of moral and political thought, social contract is no longer perceived as a historical fact. Today it is obvious that the contractual original emergence of organized society constitutes a fiction. And were it not a fiction, its persuasiveness would be dubious anyway; there is no clear reason, Rousseau's disclaimers notwithstanding, why the contract would bind anyone but those who had entered it. That is why the divine will constitutes today the only claimed heteronomous justification of major influence, and I will limit my discussion of heteronomy to the alleged divine orders.

Recognition of the divine command as the source of moral norms is persuasive for many believers. This recognition means, however, different things within different religious philosophies. In particular, it ranges from Calvin's explicitly blind obedience—"the will of God is the highest rule of justice; so that what He wills must be considered just for this very reason, because He wills it,"[1]—to a strong or weak presumption that divine orders are right. In its strong version, the presumption is irrebutable. But this version does not necessarily constitute a tautology: in the view rooted in Plato's *Euthyphro* and acclaimed by many theologians, "God wills the right because it is right, and that what is right is so, not merely because he wills it;"[2] thus, the rightness is logically independent of his will.[3] In its weak version, this is a tentative presumption only; since for most of us it is hard to have a ready and consistent moral response to the innumerable contingencies anyone encounters, many believers tentatively accept norms pronounced, in the name of God, by their religion, provided that those norms do not prove wrong on reflection, especially reflection generated by experience.[4]

Are the thus understood divine orders fit for objective justification of ethics? The weak, tentative presumption—we should obey divine orders unless we find them wrong—amounts to acceptance of the ultimate individual moral autonomy, that is, to virtual rejection of the religious justification. On the other hand, the unconditional, blind obedience provides a clear attempt at justification in the here accepted sense. The same may be claimed true of the strong, irrefutable presumption that what God orders is right.

As stressed earlier, this kind of justification constitutes a practical syllogism: "You should do what God orders; God orders 'you should do X'; you should do X." Thus, the validity of the justification depends, in particular, upon the veracity of the small premise that states the normmaking fact: God orders "you should do X." The premise implies that God, however understood, exists, and has pronounced (directly, through a prophet, or otherwise) the norm "you should do X." Claims of veracity of the thus conceived small premise abound in various religions. Needless to say, these claims often contradict one other. The Judaeo-Christian God orders that "you ought not kill," whereas Allah of the fundamentalist extremists proclaims the duty to entertain holy wars and kill infidels. And even among the claims voiced within the same denomination contradictions occur frequently.

The small premise that asserts the religious normmaking fact is always true or false, whatever behavior we substitute for X. In other words, it is always either true or false that God (exists and) has ordered us to do X. However, even though the statement has truth value, its untestability is not due to our temporary lack of knowledge, but inherent. Thus, owing to its metaphysical character, we are in a stalemate: it is impossible to assess the validity of religious justification of moral norms.

Reason

At least since the Stoics, the search for a rational foundation of ethics has been with us. But reason as the mainspring of ethics is an ambiguous notion. The Stoics, especially Zeno of Citium, perceived it as the pantheistic force governing the universe, as did Cicero two centuries later. The Scholastics treated moral norms, under the name of "natural law," as a creation of human reason reflecting the divine *lex aeterna*, and St. Thomas claimed explicitly that a "tyrannical law," by running against reason and thus "against the law of nature…is no longer a law but a perversion of law."[5] Accordingly, such laws "do not bind in conscience," that is, they justify disobedience, "except perhaps in order to avoid scandal or disturbance"[6] Grotius considered norms of natural law "a dictate of right reason which points out that an act, according as it is or is not in conformity with rational nature, has in it a quality of moral baseness or moral necessity."[7] Each of these thinkers approves, at least implicitly, the rule of recognition: we should accept those moral norms that derive from reason. Thus (the variously understood) reason becomes, in their view, the normmaking fact providing objective justification. And each of them construes a catalog of the reason-engendered norms. For instance, Cicero's list converges largely with the Roman *ius naturale*. The list of St. Thomas includes such obligations as the duty to preserve one's life, not to harm others, and to act in a rational manner. And the list of Grotius enumerates the obligation to perform contracts, to accept the absolute power of the state, and to accept the basic duties known to the civil and criminal law of his day.[8]

Kant's justification of morality became particularly influential within this tradition. In his view "all moral concepts have their seat and origin entirely *a priori* in reason."[9] Kant refers here to the pure, practical reason of any existing or imaginable "rational being," not merely to human reason.[10] Had Kant been referring just to human reason, Kantian reason would have been a peculiar characteristic of human nature; in particular, had Kant been referring to human reason embedded in the brain, Kantian reason would have been reduced to the empirical human nature—an implication which Kant emphatically rejects.[11]

By "moral concepts" Kant means here moral judgments, especially moral norms. Our knowledge of these norms is of the most certain kind; they are synthetic propositions known *a priori*. Kant's epistemology treats empirical knowledge as inferior; our perceptions provide us only with appearance of things, not with knowledge of "things in themselves," that is, of the real, "noumenal" world. There is only one part of the noumenal world truly accessible to our cognition, and this is our nonempirical "transcendental self," that is, our pure practical reason from which the moral norms flow. This is why we do know these norms genuinely, in themselves, and thus we cannot but accept them.

What are these norms? Kant includes here only those norms (but not all the norms) that fit his venerated principle of universality: "Act only according to the maxim by which you can at the same time will that it should become a universal law."[12] Then he lays down a number of the norms to be accepted. One of them constitutes the "supreme practical principle:...Act so that you treat humanity, whether in your own person or in that of another, always as an end and never as a means only."[13] Many other norms follow. They impose the duty to unconditionally tell the truth, to fulfill promises, especially repay loans, to benevolently promote the well-being of others and to respect their freedom, dignity, and property, to be sincere in friendship, to refrain from suicide, and to develop one's abilities.[14] Accepting these norms as universally binding is an objective necessity for a rational being; what they demand are "actions inexorably commanded by reason;"[15] which implies that denial of any of these norms, by running counter to reason, is impossible.

There is a problem with this justification. Kant's assertions, as well as those of the Stoics, Scholastics, or Grotius, may be true. In particular, it may be true that there exists pure practical reason, that it is the seat and source of ethics, that moral norms are synthetic propositions *a priori*, and that, since they are the only part of the noumenal world truly accessible to our cognition, we do know them with certainty, as things in themselves. However, these assertions may be false as well. If they are true, they provide a valid justification in the here accepted sense. On the other hand, if they are false, not only do they fail as objective justifications, but, as various critics claim, they constitute sheer tautologies.[16] Unfortunately, all these assertions are as metaphysical as the belief in divine orders as the source of ethics. Accordingly, we are unable to assess the validity of Kantian (or Zeno's, or de Groot's) "reason" as justification.

To be sure, Kant's is not the final attempt on the part of those who try to justify an ethical system by command of reason. Today, moral thinkers who assert that reason tells us what we ought to do, abstain from Kantian epistemology. Some, partially adhering to Kant's line of thought, try to do the impossible and prove that persons who reject moral principles of freedom and well-being commit a self-contradiction; these persons deprive everyone, including themselves, of conditions necessary for rational action, that is, for any action, since all human action is, in this view, always rational.[17] Others refer to various versions of the ideal observer theory. For instance, according to Brandt's view, in order to be justified, that is, to be considered rational, a moral norm must be most critically appraised in light of empirical fact and logic, that is, with optimal use of all the available relevant information.[18] Nonetheless, despite the merits of his forceful plea for rationality, it would be difficult to accept Brandt's stand here.

The merits of the plea are obvious. The use of the best available information and sound thinking is often helpful in determining what ought to be done. In particular the information can help to eliminate false belief in the occurrence of a normmaking fact (for example, belief in the original emergence of organized society through a social contract), or belief in a false factual premise for moral inference within a primary moral system (such as belief in the horrors caused by witches).[19] And, very importantly, the information can help to anticipate practical consequences of the norms under consideration. But, however useful this rationality in scrutinizing moral norms may be, it does not amount to their objective justification in the sense accepted in this book; indeed, Brandt's rationality can be easily (and wisely) recommended by a moral skeptic. As indicated earlier, a high degree of persuasiveness of the normmaking fact (and of its rule of recognition) is a prerequisite for the validity of any claimed justification. Whether critical use of reason fulfills this prerequisite is at least dubious. Unless one agrees with the strong version of "ethical universalism" rebutted earlier, the compelling appeal of factual knowledge and critical thinking underlying a moral choice is clearly limited in human societies, even those whose way of life has been shaped by Western civilization. This is so since hardly any society is made up of intellectuals ready to adopt, under "compulsion-by-lucid-ideas,"[20] thoughtfulness and logic as the normmaking fact. And even the best educated and most critical individuals are not necessarily ready either. Having internalized differential ultimate moral principles, many of them can utter moral norms unacceptable for many others who may be equally well informed and equally critical.

Cognitivism: The Truth Value of Moral Judgments

Cognitivists claim that some moral judgments, especially some moral norms, are true. Again, their justifying reasoning constitutes a simple syllogism: "We accept true statements; norm X is a true statement; we accept norm X." To be sure, this is a fully developed logical structure; cognitivists of various shades stress only the normmaking fact expressed in the small premise (e.g., "the norm 'you ought not kill' is true"), and then draw the conclusion without spelling out the rule of recognition expressed in the large premise. Nonetheless, implicitly, the rule of recognition is always there. As I have noted earlier, if a moral judgment is true, its veracity provides its justification in the strongest sense; the way our mind works compels us to accept statements we are convinced to be true. In other words, the way our mind works makes rejection of what we hold true virtually impossible.[21]

Cognitivists admit a genuine, factual existence of moral goodness or oughtness, and thus perceive moral judgments as statements of fact. Thus, they do not abandon the correspondence theory of truth. But how do they proceed to establish the truth value of moral judgments? Plato's ontological cognitivism provides one way, whereas modern, analytical intuitionism provides another. I will discuss both of them in turn.

In the world of Platonic ideas there are moral values, all of them culminating in the idea of the good. Since the ideas exist, and they exist more genuinely than appearances known as physical bodies, the idea of the good does exist in the very real sense. Thus, moral judgments, especially on what is or is not good, have truth value. They are true if what they say corresponds with the idea of the good. And their veracity can be found out, but only by sages who, having mastered the art of intellectual intuition, are able to visualize the ideas.

This view has had an impact on ethical thinkers of various persuasions. Most recently, it has influenced the ethical thought of phenomenologists, and of those existentialists who apply the phenomenological method to the analysis of the world.

"Phenomenology" denotes a variety of notions that shift, sometimes elusively, from one phenomenologist to another. Even the views of such founders of the doctrine as Husserl and Scheler had been changing dramatically. Nonetheless, there is a common core to these views, and there are, within this common core, a few points of consequence for this writing.

One of these points is the existence not only of material, but also of ideal objects. Both kinds exist independently of anyone's consciousness; in the ever-evolving ontology of Husserl, the existence of the latter became largely Platonic. In the world of ideas, there do exist, among others, moral values, especially moral oughtness. How do we discover the existence of ideal objects? We do so in a manner peculiar to the phenomenological discovery of any object—by intuitive insight, free from conceptual presuppositions, into the essence of the object, that is, into its characteristics without which it would be an object of a different kind; or, in other words, into those characteristics that constitute the essentialist definition of the object. The intuitive insight becomes highly emotional whenever it refers to such ideal objects as moral values or moral oughtness.

We report this intuitively accessible existence of moral values in axiological judgments, such as "X is good" or "X is evil." And we report the existence of moral oughtness in moral norms. This means that the axiological judgments and the norms have truth value. "The judgment 'X is good' is true if, and only if, in phenomenological reality, X is good."[22] And the norm "you ought respect human dignity" is true if, and only if, in phenomenological reality, one ought to respect human dignity.

Thus, in the Platonic tradition, the claim of veracity of moral judgments has been rooted in elaborate, idealistic ontology. Early in this century, however, another kind of intuitionism came to be well established in moral philosophy. A group of British commonsense realists made a similar claim of veracity, but without referring to grand-style ontological speculation. Their theory—analytical intuitionism—gained, for a few decades, the dominant position in ethical thought.

There are two versions of the doctrine. Some of its proponents, following the lead of G.E. Moore, advocate the axiological version. They assert the truth value of judgments that stipulate what is good, and they preceive the goodness as an indefinable, nonnatural, intuitively apprehensible property of acts and persons. The goodness thus understood serves as a premise for derivation of what ought to be done, that is, of moral norms. The majority of analytical intuitionists, however, accept the deontological stand, and I will deal with that majority now.

There are differences among the deontologists, but all of them treat "ought" as an indefinable, primitive term, in a manner similar to Moore's treatment of "good." Consequently, they treat moral norms as "first and irreducible," that is, they do not derive the norms from axiological judgments. They simply ascribe underivative truth value to moral norms, and they claim that the obvious veracity of true norms can be immediately grasped by intuition. In contrast with phenomenologists, they understand the intuition as a rational rather than emotional insight, "an act of moral thinking."[23] This act consists in apprehension of true moral norms and principles—a true moral norm, even though synthetic, is as "self-evident...as a mathematical axiom or the validity of inference."[24] Thus, true moral norms do not require any empirical evidence beyond the intuitive insight; they are "evident without any need of proof,"[25] and, in this sense, they are known to be true *a priori*.

What are those true norms? Analytical intuitionists cluster them into various moral systems. Some of these systems are made of a few general principles. For instance, Sidgwick's self-evident principles include the obligation to maximize one's own pleasure and happiness, present and future, and to benevolently and equally maximize the pleasure and happiness of any other individual.[26] On the other end of the spectrum, we find the detailed system developed by Ross. His catalog of the obviously true norms is longer than Sidgwick's, and the norms impose obligations very different from those prescribed by Sidgwick's hedonistic version of utilitarianism. Unlike Sidgwick, Ross sets out to build his system by tentatively following the moral views generally accepted by those thoughtful and mature; then he refines these views. Consequently, he accepts, largely in accord with common sense, a plurality of ultimate norms and obligations. The obligations he lists include keeping promises and telling the truth, being just, promoting intellect and virtue, not harming others and compensating wrongs done, helping benefactors and returning services rendered.[27] When addressing a specific circumstance, norms imposing these obligations easily conflict with each other; that is why these norms are only prima facie true, and only balancing the conflicting prima facie obligations may bring us to the apprehension of the true, specific norms to be applied.[28]

Both versions of intuitionism—Platonic and analytical—have been harshly criticized. This is, since the 1950s, particularly true of the latter version. Its ontological and epistemological foundations, as well as its method and logic, have been challenged, and the challenges have undermined much of its appeal.

One major attempt at its refutation claims the doctrine's incompatibility with the diversity of moral views. Not only moral views of various groups of "thoughtful and mature" individuals, but also the views of the intuitionists themselves conflict with one another; the Sidgwick vs. Ross discrepancy provides just one such instance. How can moral norms intuited by anyone be true, and obviously so, if they contradict the obviously true norms intuited by others? In rejoinder, the intuitionists point out that errors in cognition, which occur in any area, factual or normative, are responsible for moral contradictions. These errors result from immaturity or flawed thinking: "the appreciation of an obligation is…only possible for a developed moral being," and, "owing to a lack of thoughtfulness, even the best men are blind to many of their obligations."[29] As mentioned earlier, Plato also claimed that only sages may be able to grasp Ideas.

Other challenges come from various empirically oriented moral philosophers. Those of them who adhere to logical positivism are inclined to limit not just scientific knowledge, but the body of meaningful statements, to intersubjectively testable propositions.[30] Clearly, assertions of the intuitionist doctrine are beyond that demarcation line, and the intuitionists not only admit that their stand is, in this sense, nonempirical,[31] but they also explicitly reject this version of empiricism; thus, in their view, by accusing them of being nonempiricist, the empiricist challenge simply begs the question.[32] Other, less radical empirical critics, most notably J.L. Mackie, complain about what they perceive to be major oddities of the doctrine. The doctrine's queerness lies, first, in the mysterious faculty of intuition. This faculty engenders another mystery— the ability to know *a priori* true synthetic moral judgments. These judgments refer to still another enigma—the nonnatural, indefinable properties, such as Ross's oughtness (or Moore's goodness).[33] The assertion that oughtness, goodness, wickedness, rights, and obligations belong to "the furniture of the world," is, in the critics' view, plainly false, a philosophical fancy. Thus, the intuitionist doctrine—in its modern as well as Platonic version—constitutes an error, even though the error is well "embedded in ordinary moral thought and language."[34]

To make their case stronger, critics of the intuitionist perspective have tried to explain why the error is well embedded. The explanation, partially indebted to Hume, refers to the tendency of our mind to project our own feelings on their objects, and thus to objectify (and often reify) the feelings; when the objects are inanimate, the projection is known, in fine arts and literature, as "pathetic fallacy."[35] The projected feelings constitute a variety, and ethical experiences are among this variety; our tendency to project ethical experiences is reflected by moral (and legal) language.[36]

The persistence with which we objectify moral evaluations is sometimes explained by the manner of their acquisition. As indicated earlier, we acquire them in the process of learning; the society we live in "showers" each of us with moral evaluations, and the evaluations, especially the norms, have an authoritative tone.[37] That is why they impress us as being real, emerging from all around and above. No wonder that a person so impressed feels, when experiencing a thus acquired evaluation, "as if there were somewhere in space, high above us, a firm and categorical prescription or proscription...and that those at whom the prescriptions and proscriptions seem directed remain in a peculiar state of being constrained, bound by duty.... This is where we should look for the source and psychological explanation of the belief, common among all peoples, in the objective, everlasting and universal validity of the relevant 'laws.'"[38] And the explanation should, in the critics' view, help to convince everyone that the belief is false.

The explanation may be convincing, but it does not amount to falsi-
fication of the intuitionist claims. The claims can be, in accord with the
"error theory...all false."[39] But, despite their queerness and vagueness, they can be true as well. They are embedded in a peculiar kind of
ontology—Platonic, or common sense ontology of Moore, Sidgwick,
and Ross. Like religious or Kantian assertions of normmaking facts,
they cannot possibly be proved or disproved, and, owing to their metaphysical character, they constitute another attempt at justification, the
validity of which seems indeterminable.

On the Road to Skepticism?

We opened our search by establishing a way to resolve the problem
of justification. The way consisted in application of three criteria of
validity to various attempted justifications. Once again, the criteria were:
the logic of any attempted justification, its persuasiveness, and, if the
ocurrence of a claimed normmaking fact is testable, empirical evidence
to test the claim. Accordingly, we proceeded to check, by application of
these criteria, all the major attempted justifications. What has been the
outcome of this procedure? Did we corroborate at least one justification? Or did we rebut all claimed justifications and thus confirm the
stand of moral skeptics?

One category of the claimed normmaking facts is testable; this is
human nature reduced to an empirical indicator. Various attempts to
confirm the occurrence of the testable normmaking facts have been made.
However, all of them ended in rebuttal. This implies that no empirical
objective justification is within our reach; which provides a considerable degree of support for the stand of moral skeptics.

On the other hand, those justifications that rest on untestable
normmaking facts cannot be refuted; and this, by contrast, precludes
the acceptance of the skeptical conclusion. Thus, due to the untestability
of various normmaking facts, we are at a stalemate. There is nothing
illogical in assuming that these facts—divine orders, noumenal reason,
Platonic ideas, nonnatural properties—are with us, and, for many of
those who so assume, they do have persuasive power. However, since
the occurrence of these facts cannot be tested, the issue is indeterminable and the stalemate may be hopeless.

This may, but does not have to be the case. Various metaphysical
beliefs are an historical circumstance, and thus they come and go. His-

tory and anthropology provide us with instances: animist orders, demands of ancestors' souls, of totems, shamans, tutelary spirits. These beliefs, untestable but logically viable, were most persuasive in the past of many societies, and thus served as claimed justifications of various moral norms. But the beliefs eventually disappeared, and so did, through desuetude, the justifications they were supposed to provide.

The same may happen to at least some of the untestable normmaking facts under discussion; indeed, decline of the belief that those facts occur may be going on before our eyes. However strong Kant's impact on our moral thinking might have been, few philosophers and even fewer nonphilosophers believe today in "things in themselves" and synthetic propositions *a priori*; and rejection of these notions entails rejection of noumenal *a priori* reason as a normmaking fact. Similarly, the truth value of moral judgments was widely accepted in moral philosophy over half a century ago, under the impact of British analytical intuitionists. But their stand, originally dominant, lost much of its appeal in the changing climate; today, the inclusion of moral values in the "furniture of the world" is increasingly out of philosophical fashion.

Divine will—understood as orders demanding blind obedience or as orders presumed right beyond refutation—has been the untestable normmaking fact with particularly widespread appeal, owing to the lasting appeal of religion. But, despite the persistence of religiosity, desuetude of religious justification of ethics may occur. The doctrine of human moral autonomy, beholden largely to Protestant and, especially, Kantian thought, is increasingly taking hold over the mind of modern man, religious or not. And further growth and spread of the emotional appeal of this doctrine can remove altogether from future societies, even the religious ones, the persuasive force of the alleged divine orders.

Thus, eventually, all untestable justifications may disappear—also those founded on lasting beliefs. This would vindicate the view of moral skeptics. To be sure, we are far from that kind of vindication. Even though such metaphysical justifications as noumenal reason, Platonic ideas, or nonnatural properties have today limited impact only, divine will is widely perceived as the source of moral norms. And, even if sometime the doctrine of moral autonomy wins over human societies, the vindication of skepticism would not be entirely safe. Finding out that, in the world as we know it, no normmaking fact fit for the justification has been demonstrated does not definitively prove that none exists: a testable and persuasive normmaking fact might be newly conceived and its ocurrence confirmed in the future. Only with this reservation would the disappearance of all untestable justifications bring the problem of justification to its skeptical solution.

Notes

1. Quoted after Brandt 1959: 68.
2. Ginsberg 1965: 41.
3. See also Russell 1962: 38, 60; for a different view, cf. Ayer 1984: 20.
4. This is not a full enumeration of the meanings in which divine will is recognized as the source of ethics. Sometimes, the recognition comes from belief in the divine nature of the world and man; here, the nature as the mainspring of ethics converges with God. It converges, in particular, in view of those pantheists who reduce the world to God (but not of those who, like Strato, reduce God to the world, thus approaching the materialist stand), and of those ontological idealists who believe in the God-devised universe pervaded by ethical values, that is, in the world consisting of both what is and what ought to be. On the religiously understood natural law which reflects the divine reason, see 59, *infra*.
5. St. Thomas 1945: 760 (qu. 92, art. 1) and 784 (qu. 95, art. 2). This doctrine of natural law has been accepted by some Neo-Aristotelians and by Neo-Thomists of today. For its particularly influential defense see MacIntyre 1984 (and MacIntyre 1959, for an early articulation of his view) who accepts the doctrine on both basic and teleological grounds. When dealing with the latter, he blasts the heirs of Enlightenment, especially rationalists, Kantians, emotivists, existentialists, and utilitarians, for their success in eliminating objective justification of morality from the mind of the modern man. He believes that the elimination has caused the increasing moral breakdown of modern societies, that is, "the failure of the Enlightenment project." For the most recent articulation of a similar view see John Paul II 1994.
6. St. Thomas 1945: 795 (qu. 96, art. 4).
7. Grotius 1853, book I, ch. I(X).
8. I benefited here from a critical analysis of these catalogs by Lande 1959: 541–43.
9. Kant [1785] 1959: 28.
10. Moral law "holds not merely for men but for all rational beings as such"(*ibid.*, 24); "the command 'Thou shalt not lie' does not apply to men only, as if other rational beings had no need to observe it. The same is true for all other moral laws"(*ibid.*, 5).
11. Kant's is a radically deterministic view of the empirical human nature. Only our pure practical reason—the *a priori* producer of moral judgments—works in a manner free of causal constraints, and thus, by providing us with freedom of choice, makes us morally responsible. That is why "the ground of obligation...must not be sought in the nature of man..., but sought a priori solely in the concept of pure reason, and [no] precept which rests...on empirical grounds...may be called...a moral law"(*Ibid*).
12. *Ibid.*, 39. This and the preceding quotations come from Kant's *Foundations of the Metaphysics of Morals* which appeared in Germany in 1785. But the epistomology

underlying that book had been rooted in his *Kritik der reinen Vernunft* published, in its first edition, in 1781.

13. Kant 1959: 47.
14. Ibid., *passim.*
15. *Ibid.,* 24.
16. In the view of those critics, it is easy to ascribe the meaning one looks for to such vague expressions as "right reason," "rational nature," or "pure practical reason." Thus Kant, as well as Cicero, St. Thomas, Grotius, and many others, first accept intuitively the norms they intend to justify, and then ascribe to those vague expressions the meaning which encompasses the accepted norms; accordingly, they conclude that the norms are embedded in man's rational nature, pure reason, etc. Apparently, they are unaware of the circular character of their reasoning. But the meaning they ultimately ascribe to those expressions "reflects merely the current ethos of their own environment" (Lande 1959: 541-43). Also Kant's "maxims which he had learned from his virtuous parents were those which had to be vindicated by a rational test" (MacIntyre 1984: 44).
17. Of course, I refer here to Alan Gewirth's numerous works, especially his *Reason and Morality* and *Human Rights,* both highly influential and widely criticized.
18. Brandt 1979, esp. ch. 10. For an earlier, different version of Brandt's stand, see 1959: 244-52, 259-64.
19. Cf. 22, 26, *supra.*
20. The expression comes from Gellner 1992: 10.
21. For a qualification of this stand see ch. 1, n. 11, *supra.*
22. Kalinowski 1967: 208.
23. Prichard 1949: 16.
24. Ross, W.D. 1930: 29. Ross claims here intuitive apprehension of general norms—he calls them general principles—whereas other deontologists stress intuiting individual norms which prescribe specific actions.
25. *Ibid.*
26. Sidgwick 1962: 9, 380-82.
27. Ross, W.D. 1939: 75-77, 87.
28. Ross, W.D. 1930: 19-47; 1939: 83-86.
29. Prichard 1949: 9-10, n.1.
30. This view may underlie, in particular, the later criticism by A.J. Ayer. To be sure, having moderated his views expressed in *Language, Truth and Logic* over half a century ago, he does not refer (or, at least, does not explicitly refer) to the intrinsically untestable character of the intuitionist doctrine. He argues: "My reason for ruling this theory out is frankly that I do not understand it. What puzzles me is [the view of some critics] that the belief in there being objective values is merely false, as if the world might have contained such things, but happens not to, just as it happens not to contain centaurs or unicorns. Whereas I think that…the champions of objective values have failed to make their belief intelligible" (1984: 20, 33). It is difficult to read from these words and their context whether, and to what degree, Ayer's challenge is ultimately embedded in his original acceptance of verifiability theory of descriptive meaning.
31. The doctrine is nonempirical in the here stipulated sense, but intuitionists may consider themselves "empiricists" in a different meaning; they may claim that they empirically verify moral judgments by the intuitive insight.
32. Cf. Brandt 1959: 189.

33. "If there were objective values, then they would be entities or qualities or relations of a very strange sort, utterly different from anything else in the universe. Correspondingly, if we were aware of them, it would have to be by some special faculty of moral perception or intuition, utterly different from our ordinary ways of knowing everything else" (Mackie 1977: 38).
34. *Ibid.*, 48–49.
35. *Ibid.*, 42; cf. also Ayer 1984: 33.
36. We say that this or that *is* a person's right or duty. We speak about ourselves *having* rights and duties, *being bound* by obligations, *being* good or wicked or virtuous. And so we speak about human behavior: it *is* right, fair, wrong, unjust. These expressions show how we objectify our moral experiences, in particular our feelings of duties and rights. And, since moral norms express these feelings, we tend to perceive the norms as "binding" ourselves and others in the most objective manner.
37. 5–6, *supra.*
38. The quotation comes from Petrażycki, whose elaborate view of the issue was first published in 1909 (Petrażycki 1959-60, vol.1: 49-62; the quotation: pp. 59-60, 66. Cf. also vol. 2: 21, and, on aesthetic projections see Petrażycki 1985: 471-75). For similar views expressed later see, in particular, Alf Ross 1933, chapter 7.
39. Mackie 1977: 35.

4

Criticism: Human Nature
as the Source of Hope

The foregoing comments bring about an important conclusion: human nature, at least as understood here, does not justify human rights. However, human nature is, for a reason not as yet debated, a source of hope; due to a peculiar, empirical characteristic of human nature, the idea of human rights can be universally accepted by all nations and all governments as well. This peculiar characteristic consists in human polymorphism—the innate plasticity of human behavior and, subsequently, the potential diversity of social behavior learned by individuals and societies. Owing to this characteristic, the implementation of human rights can successfully occur, irrespective of whether the implementation is objectively justified. Which easily brings about criticism of the perennial search for justification. If the plasticity of human behavior makes implementation of human rights feasible, the search for justification is not really important and may well be forgotten. We ought to do what is right if doing so is feasible rather than to speculate on why doing so is right. This stand has been forcefully voiced by various social philosophers, and it has been at least implicitly accepted by many lawyers dealing with human rights from a pragmatic perspective. To make this criticism clear, I will elaborate on polymorphism.

Human Genetic Program: Stanisław Ossowski's
Manichean Predilections

The mosquito is an automaton. It can afford to be nothing else. There are only about one hundred thousand nerve cells in its tiny head, and each one has to pull its weight. The only way to run accurately and successfully through a life cycle in a matter of days is instinct, a sequence of rigid behaviors programmed by the genes...

73

The channels of human mental development, in contrast, are...variable. Rather than specify a single trait, human genes prescribe the *capacity* to develop a certain array of traits. In some categories of behavior, the array is limited and the outcome can be altered only by strenuous training—if ever. In others, the array is vast and the outcome easily influenced.[1]

As these words imply, the human genetic program provides us with considerable plasticity: under the impact of different environments, human individuals and human societies can learn to respond in a variety of ways to identical discrete stimuli.

Of course, this flexibility varies from one kind of behavior to another. For some behaviors, the degree of flexibility is, indeed, minor, if any. For instance, if a human group attempted to introduce the habit of four limb locomotion, abandoning of children by mothers, eliminating the use of articulate language, or comprehensively imitating the distinctive social arrangements of gorillas or rodents, "their effort would soon collapse and they would revert to fully human behaviors."[2] To put it broadly, whenever our culture demands of us any responses that go beyond the limits of our phylogenetic program, the stubborn biological necessity will resist these demands and eventually "revise the culture." In this sense it is obviously true that, as the metaphor goes, our genes "hold culture on a leash."[3]

But, for the majority of human behaviors, especially emotional responses, the leash is long. For instance, there is genetic ground for the development of the neurophysiology necessary for speech, play, sexuality. But there is plasticity in the kind of language, play, and sexual expressions that are learned.

The plasticity is particularly marked with respect to moral experience and the conduct which that experience generates. The human phylogenetic program provides all of its carriers with the ability to acquire moral experiences. The ability materializes in the course of the ontogenetic development of human mind: in the process of maturation, we learn to experience right and wrong, and rights and duties of ourselves and of others.[4] But, as with language or play, there is enormous flexibility in the contents of the moral feelings we acquire, and the resulting evaluative judgments we express in word and action. Owing to variable environment and the ensuing differential learning, not only individuals within the same society, but also the same individuals at different moments, respond to identical behavior with different evaluations. And, most importantly for this writing, different groups and societies respond to identical behavior with sometimes dramatically differing distributions of evaluations. Consequently, patterns of conduct generated by moral experiences vary at the individual level, from one individual to another, and from society to society. In other words, there is in each of us and, consequently, in each human society, the potential for experiencing the rightness of rescuing and killing, caring and torturing, loving and hating.

There is nothing new about this polymorphism. People have always been aware of it,[5] thought of it with a mixture of concern and bewilderment, and have been looking for its explanation. Why does the dualism of right and wrong cut across the hearts of human individuals and across every society? For thousands of years, mythology and religion have claimed to have answered the question: supernatural forces sow virtue and evil in the human mind. There are among those forces the good spirits and demons of pagan myths, various versions of the ormuzds and ahrimans in oriental religions, eons of the gnostics. In Stanisław Ossowski's words, spelled out in his "Manichean Predilections,"

> According to the Manichaean doctrine, man was created by Satan from components of light which Satan had stolen from the Light God and from components of the everlasting satanic darkness... Zoroaster's creed, even though somewhat less pessimistic about the creation of man, looked, nonetheless, at the emergence of human nature as an outcome of conflicting good and evil forces. This religious dualism has strong psychological support. This is probably the reason why it has been so clearly expressed in Judaism and Christianity. It is easy to believe that man has been created by both the radiant Ahur Mazda and the dark Angra Maniu, and to believe in Satan's contribution to the formation of human nature when one can so often observe, on the part of the same person, symptoms of cunning egoism and altruistic sacrifice, inclination to benevolence and hatred.[6]

Individual Diversity: From Warsaw to Treblinka, 1942–43

> *To the memory of Stanisław Lubowiecki, Halina*
> *Maria Bukowiecka, Irena Lubowiecka, Jan*
> *Pietrzak, Zofia Klimontowicz, Anna and Jerzy*
> *Lubomirski, Henryka Filipkowska and Janina*
> *Roszak—the Christian Poles who helped my*
> *mother and me to escape from the Warsaw*
> *Ghetto and sheltered us in 1942–1945.—J.G.*

As indicated above, this diversity manifests itself in the behavior of individuals and societies. At the individual level it does so, first, as intrapersonal variation, that is, variation in behavior of the same individual: anyone's morally relevant behavior ranges from his or her most righteous to most wrongful act, with varying frequencies of these acts scored along the scale. And, second, it shows as interpersonal variation: the ranges and frequencies differ from one individual to another. For someone who has been shifting between the most sacrificial altruism and sadistic murder, the range is very long; but only rarely is anyone's highest or lowest end score, not to speak of both, that extreme. The frequencies differ from person to person as well, with the central tendency shifting from the top to the bottom of the scale. In rare cases is the central tendency at the top or at the bottom; and if, in any of those rare cases, the top or the bottom score marks extreme righteousness or extreme wrongfulness, we face a truly exceptional individual—a "saint" consistently displaying utmost benevolence or, respectively, a consistently vicious wrongdoer.

The more peaceful, well-ordered and cohesive a society is, the milder the intra- and interpersonal ethical variation. With few opportunities for extremes, the ranges are limited. Also the frequencies tend to display uniformly normal distribution. On the other hand, the extremes become striking and the distributions skewed in periods of crisis. "Wartime experiences are particularly rich in this respect," asserts Ossowski in the "Manichaean Predilections." The essay was written in 1943, in Nazi-occupied Warsaw. This was a place and time of unique upheaval—a nearly natural experiment for the study of ethical polymorphism. In Ossowski's words, "we have seen genuine heroism giving way to squalid cowardice, exuberant feeling of one's dignity capitualting to concern about bread...people whose most brutal cruelty mingled with tenderness for their friends, family, children, even children of others."[7]

Even though ultimately aimed at differences among societies, these words focus on intrapersonal variation. But Warsaw of 1943 also constituted a dramatic display of interpersonal contrasts between members of the same, and, even more so, of different ethnic groups.

The Nazi terror reached its peak in Poland, especially in Warsaw; it exceeded by far the events in any occupied Western European country. Warsaw was partially destroyed in 1939, its Jewish quarters disappeared in 1943, the rest of the city was nearly totally levelled and 200,000 lives were lost in the 1944 uprising. From 1939 until 1944, arrests, killings, torture, and deportations to concentration camps never ceased, manhunts were conducted to supply Germany with slave labor, and mass executions were carried out in the streets. But 1943, when Ossowski's words were written, was more than that. It was the climax of the Holocaust which meant, for over 400,000 inhabitants of the Warsaw Ghetto, the killing of those "untransportable," especially the old, on the spot; the transporting of the majority from the *Umschlagplatz* to the gas chambers of Treblinka, and the shooting dead or burning alive of the rest during the Ghetto uprising of 1943. All this was a part of a broader scheme. Altogether, speaking of the two ethnic groups only, three million Polish Jews perished during the World War II, that is, about one half of all the victims of the Holocaust, as well as three million Christian Poles.

These were the conditions under which extremes of behavior surfaced dramatically. On one end of the spectrum, there were the majority of SS men, Gestapo, as well as collaborators, informers and blackmailers extracting ransom from the persecuted. On the other end, there were people of the most sacrificial altruism; this was particularly true of those Christian Poles (and Ossowski was among them) who, despite capital punishment as the mandatory sanction, were helping and hiding Jews.[8]

It is difficult to say, how many of those people were acting at the (highest or lowest) end of the otherwise not entirely extreme intrapersonal range, and how many of them could be classified as consistent moral extremes. But, under such circumstances, the extremes—the "saints" and the scoundrels—do emerge with unusual clarity.

Let us start with the former. Janusz Korczak, a well-known Warsaw physician and writer,[9] devoted his life to the care of orphans. In 1911, he organized the Children's Home for Jewish orphans which he lived in, directed, and maintained by appealing to philantropists. In 1940, the Children's Home was forced to move into the Warsaw Ghetto, and Korczak spent the following two years there, making an unusual effort to provide for the children and to protect them. On June 26, 1942, he wrote in his diary: "I don't make social calls. I go to beg for money, foodstuff, an item of information, a lead."[10] Igor Neverly, his Christian friend,[11] describes their last encounter and its aftermath:

> In July 1942, when it was becoming obvious that the ghetto was marked for liquidation, Maryna Falska[12] made a last attempt to save Korczak...everything was scrupulously organized—a German identity card in an assumed name, a safe room prepared by Falska on the periphery of Warsaw. I went to the ghetto on a pass for a water and sewage system inspector who, on his way back, was to take with him a locksmith working on the ghetto territory.

It is difficult to describe the psychological shock experienced by any normal man in this sinister quarter...[Korczak] looked ill, wasted, stooping. At sixty-four, his health was wrecked: at the expense of stupendous daily effort he was finding food, medicines and clothes.... I explained that now there was only a single chance to save a few from perishing.... If [he] would break up the boarding school, some of the children and teachers would perhaps have a chance to escape beyond the walls. Let him order that, and come away at once with me.

He looked at me as though disappointed with me, as though I had proposed a betrayal or an embezzlement. I wilted under his gaze and he turned away, saying quietly but not without reproach in his voice: "You know, of course, why Zalewski was beaten up..."

Piotr Zalewski...has been janitor and in charge of central heating in the Children's Home for twenty years. When the order for removal came, Zalewski wanted to go to the ghetto, too. Wolańska, who for many years had run the laundry in the Home, went with a similar application to the Nazi police. Her they merely kicked out, but to Zalewski they administered a bestial remainder that he was an Aryan...

So Korczak recalled Zalewski with an obvious though unformulated reproach— you see, a janitor would not leave the children because he was attached to them, and you propose that I, their tutor, their father...

On the 5th of August, 1942, began the march of the children and teachers of the Children's Home, led by Janusz Korczak and Stefania Wilczyńska.[13] Neatly clad in their best clothes they marched in fours, steadily, under their flag—the gold four-leaf clover on a field of green, as dreamed by King Matthew,[14] because green is the symbol of everything that grows—fluttering above their heads. They marched through the hushed streets of Warsaw to the *Umschlagplatz*, near the Gdańsk Railway Station. Here they were all loaded into chlorinated freight cars. The train set out for the Treblinka extermination camp.

What did the opposite extreme look like? Kurt Franz was an SS officer at Treblinka. Whether he was among those who received Korczak and his children on their arrival, nobody knows; no witnesses to their death survived. But, in general, the way of killing in Treblinka is known. Altogether up to one million people perished there, the majority in gas chambers and others shot, hanged, or tortured.[15] Only one group was temporarily spared—the "work Jews" selected for such tasks as construction and maintainance, sorting luggage brought by the inmates, removing bodies of the dead from the gas chambers and cremating them.[16]

Kurt Franz was among the most dreaded figures at the camp.[17] In the words of an inmate who arrived from Warsaw in the end of August, 1942, and was, on the same day, selected for work:

Late in the afternoon another train arrived...but [because of suffocation] 80 percent of its human cargo consisted of corpses. We had to carry them out of the train, under the whiplashes of the guards.... After a while we were ordered to form a semi-circle.... Franz walked up to us accompanied by his dog and a Ukrainian guard armed with a machine gun. We were about 500 persons. We stood in mute suspense. About 100 of us were picked from the group, lined up five abreast, marched away some distance and ordered to kneel. I was one of those picked out. All of a sudden there was a roar of machine guns and the air was rent with the moans and screams of the victims. I never saw any of these people again. Under a rain of blows from whips and rifle butts the rest of us were driven into the barracks.[18]

Franz was particularly active at the reception area for arriving inmates and at the roll-call square for the "work Jews." At the evening roll call, as stated by the West German court that convicted Franz and his cronies in 1965,

the sick, the debilitated and...those inmates who had been..."marked" by welts or wounds from floggings or other causes during that day, were separated from the others and sent to the *lazaret* for liquidation. The evening roll call was also the time when corporal punishment was administered to inmates [often] on...pretexts such as reports that the inmate had not worked hard enough [or] had failed to give the proper salute to some *Unterfuehrer*...Even while they worked, the "work Jews" were in danger of their lives.[19]

Some of the dangers were described by another "work Jew" who escaped:

It was the habit [of Franz] to leave several people behind him every time he took a stroll through the camp. He used to stand off at a distance and observe a group of workers; if by some chance somebody was not working fast enough, or simply happened not to please him, he would come over and beat him with the whip...until the blood flowed. Then he would order him to strip naked and put a bullet in his neck.[20]

And, in the words of the same German criminal court:

Mostly, when Franz made the rounds [of the camp, his dog] Barry would accompany him. Depending on his mood, Franz would set the dog on inmates who for some reason attracted his attention...Barry was the size of a calf..., he frequently bit his victims in the buttocks, in the abdomen and...the genitals...When the inmate was not very strong, the dog could knock him to the ground and maul him beyond recognition.[21]

Divergent Societies

Since social groups are aggregates of interacting individuals,[22] individual diversity of social behavior easily translates, under the impact of divergent cultural and ecological determinants, into group diversity.

Thus, distributions of various "personality traits" vary from one group to another and from one society to another.

This differential distribution gave rise, especially around the middle of this century, to a search for detection of differential "national character" understood as a distinctive, dominant modal personality of various nations, that is, a widespread central tendency in distribution of personality characteristics within each of the nations under scrutiny.[23] Understandably, this search has been inconclusive, and it has been so not only, as sometimes claimed, due to problems of measurement. The term "personality" (or "character") is extremely broad. It denotes the sum of all mental, attitudinal, and motivational characteristics of an individual, that is, a near endless catalog of traits. Consequently, it is hard to find the dominant modal personality peculiar for any nation or society; with respect to a major part of personality characteristics, there always are significant intragroup differences on the one hand, and intergroup similarities on the other. Thus, we can only look for some personality trait or traits as a peculiar, dominant characteristic of a nation or society. And only the thus focused "national character" studies—with Riesman's and Lipset's work as the two most conspicuous instances—seem to be of lasting value.

Of course, a limited number of widely experienced moral evaluations are easily among such traits. I am stressing here only a number of moral evaluations, not all of them. To be sure, efforts to grasp the whole of a society's unique ethos have been made by various thinkers. However, the search for a complete moral system as a peculiar characteristic of any society, especially of any developed society, seems nearly as hopeless as the search for its dominant modal personality. On the other hand, a limited number of moral evaluations, especially of principles grouped around a unifying moral idea, often takes hold over the majority of a tribe, nation, or group of nations. This has been the case with such moral ideas as nationalism, militarism, cult of the state, religious fundamentalism, ultimate family loyalty, cherishing hard work and individual achievement. And, in particular, this has been the case with such evaluations as principles grouped around the human rights idea— the universal equal value of human life, dignity, essential liberties, and a degree of individual well-being.

It is obviously true that, owing to human polymorphism, the dominant stand of human societies on human rights principles varies. To confirm this, it is enough to look into history and anthropology, and to compare the societies of Sparta and Periclean Athens, Nazi Germany and Switzerland, Khomeini's Iran and Norway, the Navaho and the Tiv. More importantly, owing to the plasticity of human behavior, evolution of any society, even the most oppressive one, toward acceptance of human rights principles, is feasible. The feasibility is well established by such divergent historic experiences as the unfinished but most remarkable evolution in Greece, from the barbarian cruelties of Thales' Miletus to the Golden Age of Athens; the evolution of the northernmost part of Europe from the days of the Vikings to modern Scandinavian nations; and the German evolution from Nazi Germany to the West Germany of 1989[24]—an evolution imposed from the outside, but contingent upon the preceding development from medieval Germanic tribes to the Germany of Lessing and Beethoven.

Thus, eventually, the universal implementation of the human rights idea, even though far from certain, is possible. To return to Ossowski's words written in Warsaw of 1943:

> When painful experiences befall us, when meanness of human behavior makes social relations aversive...the Manichaean doctrine of duality of human nature can be helpful. In its modern...psychological articulation, the doctrine turns into the acceptance of human polymorphism.

> The same man may be either this or that. What we have seen in [some among us] are only their...unfortunate forms which, under the circumstances, have gained the upper hand.... In other conditions, different possibilities hidden in their personalities...could have taken the upper hand, and then we would have seen these same people in entirely different roles.

> The mental potentialities on which one would like to establish a vision of the future world do occur today as well: they emerge in behavior of exceptional individuals, exceptional groups, and average individuals in exceptional states of mind. These relatively rare occurrences prove that our vision is not infeasible.... Having accepted the notion of human polymorphism, we may expect that the attitudes, today somewhat exceptional, could, in different circumstances, spread to a degree determining the new shape of the whole of social life. The problem is how to provide conditions which would tap the hidden human potential and...how to shift the central tendencies.

> The polymorphist view that human potentialities reach at least as far as even the most exceptional attitudes and behaviors...enables us to accept the optimal program without succumbing to [such illusions as] the timid faith in the innate goodness of human nature.

> Of course, accepting such a program means conscious risk-taking. Earlier generations believed that a new, better world must come irrespective of anyone's will, as

determined by the laws of history.... This feeling of certainty provided, for many individuals, a strong motivation: they were glad to fight for a cause which, they firmly believed, would win anyway. Today, we don't know whether history will move toward the forms of social life in which one would want to live.... However, since all possibilities are open, participation of any individual adds to the chances of winning the struggle.[25]

Ossowski's words are, of course, relevant for human rights struggle; the plasticity of human nature makes an effective struggle for universal acceptance and implementation of human rights feasible. In this sense, the plasticity constitutes a genuine source of hope. And here the criticism of the search for justification has real bite. It is clear how much can be achieved in terms of human ethical potential, and once that much is possible, one should fight for what ought to be done without speculating about various kinds of normmaking facts—nature, reason, divine orders or truth value of moral judgments, each of them easily conflicting with each other, and all of them conflicting with autonomous axiology.

Notes

1. Wilson 1978: 56–57.
2. *Ibid.*, 21, 23.
3. *Ibid.*, 167. For a later, more formal account, see Lumsden and Wilson 1981: 13. But that account, dangerously bold and sweeping, goes much further than my text: assuming natural selection of cultural traits, it treats the leash as "genetically prescribed tendencies to use culturgens bearing certain key features that contribute to genetic fitness."
4. Cf. 86, *infra*.
5. In Aristotle's words (used in the motto to Lipset's *Political Man*), "man, when perfected, is the best of animals, but when separated from law and justice, he is the worst of all...he is the most unholy and the most savage of animals." Then innumerable others have been returning to this issue, and most recently, an obituary quotes Max Lerner's words, summing up his life in *Who's Who in America*: "I have believed in love and work, and their linkage. I have believed that we are neither angels nor devils, but humans, with clusters of potentials in both directions. I am neither an optimist nor pessimist, but a possibilist" (*New York Times* of June 6, 1992). This notion has been elaborated five decades ago, with unique insight, by Stanislaw Ossowski, to whose views I will turn now. (For a brief description of his scholarship see his biography by Nowak 1968.)
6. Ossowski 1967: 194–95.
7. *Ibid.*
8. Ossowski, as well as his wife, Professor Maria Ossowska, not only hid Jews, they were also most active in the underground Council to Assist the Jews established in Warsaw in 1942.

9. An assimilated Polish Jew, he worked with Jewish and Christian children. One of his books for children, *King Matt the First*, was published in the U.S. in 1986.
10. Korczak, *Ghetto Diary* (1978: 150).
11. A Polish writer in whose hands Korczak deposited the *Ghetto Diary*. The following words come from Neverly's preface to Korczak's *Ghetto Diary*, 74–76.
12. Korczak's friend and disciple, manager of an orphanage for Christian children in Warsaw.
13. Korczak's closest associate at the Children's Home.
14. Or King Matt the First, the hero of one of Korczak's books, see ch. 4, n. 9, *supra*.
15. For the fullest collection of the documents see Alexander Donat, 1979. The collection contains, on pp. 296–316, detailed reasons given by the German Court of Assizes in Düsseldorf which convicted Kurt Franz and nine others on September 3, 1965, in the First Treblinka Trial (AZ-LG Düsseldorf, II-931638), and Franz Stangl on December 22, 1970, in the Second Treblinka Trial (AZ-LG Düsseldorf, XI-148/69 S).
16. Approximately 1,000 "work Jews" still alive rebelled on August 2, 1943. About 200 of them escaped on that day, and "only some 60 survived the war to tell the horror story of Treblinka" (Donat 1979: 284).
17. Among those whose cruelty seems to have matched his were: Christian Wirth (nicknamed by the inmates "Christian the Terible"), Willy Mentz ("Frankenstein"), August Miete ("Angel of Death"), and Josef Hirtreiter who specialized in killing young children, on arrival, by smashing their heads against the boxcars (*ibid.*, 271–78).
18. *Ibid.*, 152.
19. *Ibid.*, 305–6.
20. *Ibid.*, 93.
21. *Ibid.*, 312–13. On Franz's arrest (in 1959), an album with photographs from his days in Treblinka was found in his apartment. The album, named by him "Die schönsten Jahre meines Lebens" (The most beautiful years of my life) was subsequently published.
22. A stress should be here on "interacting." Of course, these words do neither attempt to reduce societies to individuals nor to challenge the independence of sociology by reducing it to simpler disciplines. To be sure, reductions of diciplines, whenever feasible, are commendable; however, reduction of everything social to the psychological or the biochemical is clearly impossible.
23. For a critical summary of these efforts see Inlekes and Levinson 1968: 418–506.
24. I speak about the Germany of 1989 rather than the Germany of today, since today's Germany also includes millions of former East Germans, that is, a population where almost all the elderly were trained exclusively under both the Nazi and Stalinist systems, whereas Stalinism was the only teacher imposed on the young. Thus, it will require time to reshape the attitudes of a significant part of the German population of today.
25. Ossowski 1967: 194, 196–97.

5

Countercriticism: The Human Rights Struggle and the Need for Justification

However convincing the preceding criticism may be, objective justification is important and so is the search for it. The importance of justification is of two kinds, pragmatic and fundamental, and I will start, rather extensively, with the former, and only then turn to the latter kind. The pragmatic importance was noted briefly in an earlier chapter; it comes from the enhanced persuasiveness of the ethical norms believed objectively justified, and the persuasiveness constitutes, in turn, a major determinant of the wide acceptance of those norms. This determinant is badly needed by those who struggle for human rights—it may help them to overcome the immense difficulty of their endeavor.

The aims of those who struggle for human rights are clear. They act, first, to spread the human rights idea in such a way that it would turn from a moral idea of some to a moral idea of many and, eventually, of all or nearly all members of the human species. And, concurrently, they fight for enactment and enforcement of human rights norms by the legal systems of all states. Thus, there are two basic components of the human rights struggle. One of them is the activities aiming at moral "contagion" of the people by the human rights experience. The other one is the road from moral acceptance to legal implementation. Both of them suffer from major impediments. Those impediments should make the importance of justification clear, and I will turn to them now.

The Difficulties of the Human Rights Struggle: Contagion

The Process of Contagious Learning

We acquire our moral experiences in the process of contagious social learning touched on briefly in the introduction. This process occurs owing to the human phylogenetic ability to sense those experiences—an ability that develops in each of us in the course of our ontogeny. How this ability develops has been the subject of a long-lasting debate. Decades ago Freud and the Freudians dominated the debate; then, following the pioneering work of Piaget and Kohlberg, cognitive-developmental psychologists became the most influential intellectual force. Piaget, Kohlberg, and their innumerable students and followers have been speculating on the stages of any human child's moral development and trying to support the speculation by empirical evidence. Despite the remarkable fruitfulness of their thought, many of their assertions are highly controversial. This is particularly true of the specification of the stages: What are the peculiar characteristics of each of them? At what age does each consecutive stage begin? Are the stages universally human or culturally determined.[1]

However controversial, Piaget's and Kohlberg's findings,[2] and the findings of their followers and critics, clearly corroborate a number of points relevant to this chapter. First, they confirm the obvious: moral experiences emerge in the human child only in the course of the child's maturation; a degree of emotional and cognitive development constitutes a necessary condition for the ability to start experiencing what is morally right and wrong.[3] Moreover, a degree of intellectual and empathic capacity is needed to comprehend a variety of morally relevant facts which, once comprehended, do influence the contents of our moral experiences and judgments.[4] There are among them such facts as the intentional or unintentional character of human actions, the motives of those who act, and the consequences of anyone's behavior under evaluation, such as the suffering of others.[5] Furthermore, comprehension and articulation of our moral evaluations is mentally demanding, and so is the ability of reaching some, however imperfect, systemic consistency among them.[6] Thus, the acquisition of moral experiences depends upon the level of maturity of the acquirer.

As indicated above, those experiences are transmitted in the process of contagious social learning. The process operates through communications addressed to each of us by surrounding individuals and groups. Among the individuals, parents precede all others. The parents barrage the child with communications on what is right or wrong and what should therefore be done or avoided. And they largely shape the early cognitive and emotional development of the child in general, and thus facilitate comprehension of morally relevant facts and moral judgments. Their moral communications come in a variety of ways. Among them are verbal persuasion, facial expressions, gestures and, in particular, example. There is use of empathy by stressing the impact of the child's behavior on others. There are reinforcements applied in the form of "persuasive instrumental learning"—rewards clearly contingent upon behavior evaluated as right, and punishments clearly contingent upon behavior evaluated as wrongdoing;[7] the former includes displays of affection, gifts, entertainment, whereas withdrawal of love, verbal rebuke, spanking, and loss of gifts and privileges are among the latter (with the relative impact of each of them subject to controversial conjectures and abundance of experimental studies).

Parental influence constitutes a major determinant of the original acquisition of moral experiences; another one is behavior of early childhood peers. Later on, others increasingly replace the parents. Peers do so from adolescence through adult life. And so do other members of the groups each of us belongs to, especially persons whom we trust and respect. Moreover, we acquire moral experiences from trusted and respected groups of which we are not members, and from public figures who serve as reference individuals. We acquire them also in symbolic encounters such as religious, judicial, or national ceremonies, and by being exposed to works of art—reading *The Grapes of Wrath* or looking at the Rotterdam War Memorial. And direct as well as vicarious reinforcement of moral experiences arranged by various groups and institutions—from distribution of prizes, titles, and decorations for acts of virtue, to punishments imposed for wrongdoing by school principals, churches, or criminal courts—supersedes persuasive instrumental learning of parental home.[8]

One important reservation must be added here; this view of moral contagion is incomplete. The process of communications described here conditions acquisition of moral experiences. However, there are also other determinants of the acquisition. These are the general life circumstances of the individuals and groups exposed to moral communications, such as their interests and needs, roles, status, mode of securing subsistence, ecological circumstance, and social problems each of them encounters. Consequently, identical moral communications bring about divergent acquisition rates among the individuals and the groups addressed. In the simplest instance, the rich rather than the poor are inclined to accept the moral value of unrestricted right of property, and the poor rather than the rich, the value of economic equality. Similarly, a colonized nation is inclined to accept the moral value of self-determination, whereas a colonial power, the value of its domination in the name of its civilizing role or the superiority of its "blood" or ideology. And, in many societies of today, women are more inclined than men to accept the moral value of sexual equality.[9]

Contingent on this reservation, all kinds of moral experiences spread in the manner described here, and so do, in particular, human rights experiences. However, the idea of human rights has, as a moral idea, some peculiar characteristics. Born in its modern form over two centuries ago, it is complex, relatively new, and still evolving. It was conceived by moral and political philosophers, and its philosophical premises are contoversial. And it is a disputed idea of political morality—it proclaims the moral superiority of some political systems over others. All these peculiarities determine the distinctive way in which experiences of human rights spread.

The distinctive way consists in an unusually pronounced role played by crusaders and groups of crusaders dedicated to the spread. First among them are moral and political philosophers who have been articulating and rearticulating the idea of human rights. Its modern articulation came with Locke and the French thinkers of the Enlightenment; its many rearticulations have been provided since then, with particular intensity in the wake of World War II, by philosophers of various persuasions, especially the Kantians, Christian philosophers, existentialists, as well as utilitarians and, in a peculiar way, the Marxists; I will return to some of their views soon. The original articulation and ongoing rearticulation turned the idea into a powerful force stimulating political action. Over two centuries ago, this force became a major determinant of the American and the French Revolutions, and it then contributed to the development of constitutional rights and liberties in liberal democracies. Now it plays a significant role in the continuing struggle against despotic governments, and it increasingly challenges economic and cultural deprivation.

Today the human rights crusaders are well organized in powerful groups. Some of the groups are governmental—democratic governments tend to support the struggle for human rights (even though the support is often selective, owing to interference of counteracting values and interests[10]). Others, such as Amnesty International, the International Committee of the Red Cross, and various religious bodies, constitute private pressure groups. And, since the struggle aims not only at moral persuasion, but also at legal implementation, lawyers, by visibly claiming and promoting legal enforcement of human rights, have played an increasingly influential role in the spread of human rights experiences. There are among them some of the great legal minds of today providing jurisprudential premises for legal action and legal decisions; sometimes, their role converges with that of the moral and political philosophers of human rights. Here there are also groups of legal experts—from those serving on the European and the Inter-American Human Rights Commission, to the International Commission of Jurists—who, by monitoring human rights violations and publicizing them, stimulate emotions of the public. And so do judges of various courts, international and domestic, by publicly pronouncing human rights in their decisions.

This role of well-organized human rights crusaders is an important characteristic of the human rights struggle; nothing similar goes on with respect to the majority of other moral ideas and norms which, like prohibitions of stealing or lying and obligations to fulfill promises, are more traditional, simpler, less divisive. But otherwise, human rights experiences spread in the way characteristic of any moral contagion; activities of the crusaders, however essential, are here only one part of this way. Some of those personally exposed to their activities acquire human rights experiences directly from them, and many more do so indirectly, through the ususal web of communications including, again, words and activities by parents, peers, schools, the media, and all the other groups and individuals who participate in the ongoing transmission of values.

Contagion and Consensus

For the widest possible acceptance of a universal moral idea, a degree of consensus is necessary among those who fight for its spread. This is true, in particular, of the human rights idea; to enhance its effectiveness, the struggle for human rights should be conducted with a shared notion of what rights are "human," and this brings about the need for their agreed upon cataloging. And, to enhance its effectiveness, the struggle should be conducted with a shared view of the relative force of each of the rights listed. However, the agreement is not there, which spells an ever-recurring dilemma for human rights proponents.

To be sure, today any norm uttered by the proponents is either among or reduces to a few basic human rights norms. These "human rights principles," impose a duty to protect a handful of the most important values underlying the idea of human rights: the universal and equal value of human life, dignity, and essential liberties, and a degree of individual well-being. However, even these principles are not fully agreed upon; they are abstract enough to be variously interperted. Accordingly, the specific human rights norms derived from any of the principles are subject to disagreement—various human rights proponents derive different rights from the same principle. Moreover, even in the view of those proponents who agree on the catalog of the rights derived, many of those rights do, without agreement on their ranking, readily clash with one another. These disagreements and clashes are an outcome of the diversity of moral views among human rights proponents.

Why diversity? The proponents constitute a variety of persons and groups beholden to diverse systems of normative ethics. To start with, they differ in their stand on the justification of the norms they utter. Depending upon that stand, any human rights principle can be perceived by its proponent as an axiom of the proponent's own independent ethical system. Or, it can be perceived as a divine order or a true moral judgment or a demand of either nature or reason. (And, of course, any lower level human rights norm can be deduced from an axiom or from one or another normmaking fact and its rule of recognition.) Accordingly, the norm protecting human life can be easily accepted as a human rights principle by a religious fundamentalist, protection of dignity by a Kantian, support of liberty and equality by a skeptical liberal, and support of well-being or struggle against suffering by a skeptical utilitarian. On the other hand, a steadfast utilitarian, a skeptical liberal, a Kantian, or a religious fundamentalist may accept the remaining norms just mentioned only if they fit, respectively, the utilitarian or liberal axioms, Kantian imperatives, or divine revelations. Hence, the emergence of underlying disagreements among human rights advocates. For instance, it may be difficult for a steadfast utilitarian to protect equality or liberty whenever their growth brings an increase of suffering. It may be difficult for an advocate of Kant's moral system to protect human life, whenever the protection infringes upon the absolute duty of telling the truth. And it may be difficult for a fundamentalist religious believer to protect those components of personal liberty which would clash with some of the prescriptions of his or her faith. In this sense, divergent views of the justification are a source of dissent among human rights proponents.

Of course, they are not the only source. Dissent occurs also among those whose views of the justification do not clash. Moral skeptics, following differential moral intuitions, accept divergent systems of normative ethics; accordingly, human rights norms defended by a neo-Marxist skeptic can differ substantially from the norms defended by a libertarian or utilitarian skeptic. Those who justify their systems by the alleged divine orders, accept different sets of commandments or interpret a common set differently. In effect, human rights norms defended by a Moslem fundamentalist, a Christian fundamentalist, or an orthodox Jew can differ substantially; and so can they differ even among believers belonging to any one of these religious groups. This is also the case with those who accept the truth value of moral judgments, and those who consider reason as normmaking fact; the former can accept as true a variety of divergent lists of human rights, and the latter can decipher the human rights commands of ("pure," "noumenal," "right") reason in a number of conflicting ways. Thus, there are major controversies among human rights proponents.

The controversies notwithstanding, the proponents also share a lot; after all, they do accept the same list of the basic human rights values and principles. This common ground enables some of them to disregard the differences, and to join forces in the common struggle. This means, in particular, disregarding differences in their view of justification; persons who promote the value of human life and dignity in the conviction that these values have been instituted by a divine order can effectively cooperate with those who perceive life and dignity as an ultimate value imposed autonomously by themselves. Thus, devout believers and moral skeptics, Kantians and intuitionists, can, and to a degree do, fight together for the basic human rights values and principles, even though they may interpret those values and assign their relative weight differently. This kind of "ecumenical" approach has made it possible for various brands of human rights crusaders to join forces; they include such individuals as Pope John XXIII and Hersh Lauterpacht, Martin Luther King and Andrei Sakharov. However, even though their cooperation has been impressive and functional, their approach is far from universal among human rights proponents. This approach is open only to those of them who are tolerant and moderate enough. And it is closed, in particular, to the fanatical extremists inclined to use and abuse the rhetoric of human rights to gain power over their societies, and then to trample the rights of their people.

The Difficulties of the Human Rights Struggle: From Moral to Legal Change

It was stressed earlier that, besides the activities aiming at moral contagion, there is also a second essential component of the human rights struggle. This is the fight for legal implementation of those rights by the states all over the globe. Of course, a degree of contagion precedes the struggle for legal implementation (which explains the title of this section); only those who have already acquired human rights experiences are genuinely driven to fight for legal change. Then the two go on concurrently. On the one hand, continuing moral contagion precipitates the spread of claims *de lege ferenda.* On the other, law, with its means of enforcement, helps to accomplish the moral demands.

The purpose to be achieved is genuine implementation—not just enactment, but also enforcement of human rights norms. Vacuous enactments of human rights abound, as well as declarations not to be enforced. They include human rights lists beautifying "constitutions" of autocratic states; the list was quite impressive in the Soviet Union in the decades preceding Gorbachev, and so it is in many autocracies of today. Also some declaratory international instruments, most conspicuously the Universal Declaration of Human Rights, were, when pronounced, perceived by their framers as a morally desired "common standard of achievement,"[11] rather than binding norms of international law; "the practical unanimity of the Members of the United Nations in stressing the importance of the Declaration was accompanied by an equally general repudiation of the idea that the Declaration imposed upon them a legal obligation to respect the human rights and fundamental freedoms which it proclaimed."[12] However, under favorable circumstances, the originally nonbinding declarations and even vacuous norms may be, and sometimes have been, of use in the struggle for the future enforcement of the rights listed.[13]

The Ways of Implementing the New Laws

There are, roughly speaking, three kinds of ways that bring about implementation of human rights in the laws of nation-states. First, there is a largely spontaneous domestic implementation—an outcome of the internal development of a nation. Second, there is forceful imposition of human rights laws on a nation by external powers. And third, there is incorporation of international human rights into the national legal system. To be sure, these ways are not quite mutually exclusive. In particular, domestic implementation is rarely, if ever, fully independent of outside determinants, such as regional or global political and economic processes, and the impact of ideas from abroad or varying levels of pressure exercised by foreign human rights groups and foreign governments. (These determinants also include decline of foreign pressure preventing human rights implementation, such as disappearance, in 1945, of Nazi pressure from occupied Europe or, more recently, of Soviet pressure from Eastern and Central Europe.) On the other hand, a forceful imposition, as well as attempts at incorporation, would be ineffective without being preceded by an internal development of cultural and economic prerequisites that makes a nation able to accept the rights imposed or the rights to be incorporated. Nonetheless, despite the overlapping, there is a clear difference in the relative impact of divergent social forces in each of the three ways.

The domestic implementation has been the oldest way. An extensive spread of human rights experiences in a nation precipitates a struggle at the national level followed eventually by an enactment of human rights norms (either within the national constitution or through the standard lawmaking process). This kind of implementation may occur by peaceful evolution, a revolution or series of revolutions, or a sequence of evolutionary changes interspersed with relatively minor revolutionary upheavals. Sweden, following the fall of its Baltic empire, comes close to the first variety; France, after 1789 to the second; and the centuries of the British development to the third.

The forceful, outside imposition constitutes a very different method. It happens rarely; societies cherishing human rights are least inclined to use force, especially force of arms. However, in 1939–45, having themselves been attacked, they did so, and then imposed human rights norms, within new democratic constitutions, on Germany, Austria and Japan, and reimposed them on the liberated nations of Western Europe.

Today, a third way plays an increasingly dominant role; this is the incorporation of international human rights into national legal systems. It means inclusion of the international law of human rights, as a "higher level law,"[14] into the laws of those nation-states where human rights have not yet been implemented. The inclusion requires, on the part of a nation-state, endowment of its inhabitants with effective domestic means of enforcement. Optimally, the means would include judicial review (if human rights are a part of the nation's written constitution), decisions of administrative courts and ombudsman's motions, and imposition of penalties and damages for infringments of human rights. They would also include supervision of police, prisons, and other places of confinement, as well as vigorous action of independent mass media able to trace infringments of rights and make them publicly known. Needless to say, an independent and impartial judiciary and independent legal profession constitute an essential prerequisite for the effectiveness of these means.[15] Clearly, the process is analogous to incorporation as known to the American constitutional doctrine, that is, inclusion of the Bill of Rights, as a higher level law, into the laws of the states; the American incorporation was a slow and wavering process, stretching from the 1890s to its virtual triumph in the 1960s.

Is there a genuine chance of a similar triumph on a wider scale—of the worldwide incorporation of international human rights law? Here major obstacles exist, and that is why worldwide incorporation is a much slower and more wavering process than its American counterpart. One obvious difficulty is that, today, populations of the nation-states make up, essentially, the whole of the human species, that is, the sum total of all cultures and economies on very different levels of development. Accordingly, worldwide incorporation, which would bring us close to the triumph of the moral and political unity of man, seems a distant hope. Other difficulties come from major problems troubling international law itself. Both kinds of obstacles will be addressed now, starting with diverse levels of development of various societies.

Incorporation and Development

As I noted in the opening chapter, there are divergent conditions for acceptance and implementation of various human rights, and they are determined largely by the society's level of development; for instance, it would be impossible to demand immediate implementation of the right to religious tolerance in a well-established theocracy or of the right to democracy in the Athens of Draco. And since, disclaimers notwithstanding, no one can reasonably expect or demand the impossible,[16] we may demand the implementation of those human rights only that fit the society's level of development. That is why we may have to wait for the worldwide incorporation of some human rights. This obstacle inhibits incorporation of traditional, political human rights. And it inhibits, more forcefully, incorporation of the later, social and economic "generation" of human rights.

One reservation must be added here. Some international agreements introduced, in addition to the political and socioeconomic rights, a new, "third generation" of claims to the already growing list—various rights of collectivities, such as all peoples' right to development itself, to peace, self-determination and free disposal of their natural wealth and resources.[17] Some of these claims are of the utmost importance, and this is particularly true of the claim for development by poor areas of the world—an issue to which I will return soon. However, even though each of these claims may constitute a well-founded moral right and, especially *de lege ferenda*, a legitimate legal right,[18] they are, as *human* rights, such an ambiguous, self-contradictory dangerous and unhelpful novelty, that it would be difficult to opt for their inclusion into the human rights catalog.[19] That is why I will discuss here only the difficulties in incorporating the first two generations of human rights—those political and socioeconomic.

The modern human rights doctrine was a product of the Enlightenment. As mentioned earlier, Locke's natural rights were few; they included right to life, liberty, and property (and property was apparently understood by him not only as wealth, but as a requisite for individual autonomy). The American Declaration of Independence rearticulated Locke's triad as the equal and unalienable right of all men to life, liberty, and the pursuit of happiness, and added the right to a representative government, and the right to abolish any governement destructive to the "rights of man." Subsequently, the French Declaration of 1789 proclaimed a more specific list: liberty to do anything that does not injure others, especially freedom of thought, religion, and expression; the right to representative and accountable government, and to resist oppression; the right to equalized apportionment of taxes; and the right to security, property, equal treatment before the law, and equal eligibility of all citizens commensurate with their capacities to "all public dignities...and employments." Furthermore, the authors of the French

Declaration proclaimed a number of rights aimed at the system of criminal justice; having rebelled against an oppressive regime, they knew that a fair criminal justice system is an essential prerequisite for the citizen's liberty, dignity, and equal treatment. Two years later the Bill of Rights was ratified in America, spelling out the rights of man "retained by the people" of the United States. Its ratification brought further extention and specification of the list: the right of assembly and to petition the government were added, and a more detailed set of claims providing for fairness of criminal law and procedure. Then, the post-Civil War constitutional amendments, having abolished slavery, proclaimed equal protection of the laws, and equal right to vote for all, irrespective "of race or color," while the civil rights legislation of the 1960s was designed to shelter these claims against private or seemingly private conduct, especially against the conduct of "private power aggregates [capable] to limit the very freedoms the Constitution has attempted to protect."[20] Womens' equal right to vote was proclaimed only in 1920. And, since the early 1800s, owing to the development of judicial review, courts have been increasingly able to influence the meaning of the items on the list.

All these developments were, essentially, limited to the traditional area of political rights (or, in a different wording to be used on the upcoming pages, of "political and civil rights."[21]) But, even within this reasonably well-established area, implementation of many such rights may be out of reach in a number of societies. This difficulty has been made particularly clear with respect to one political human right of crucial importance—the right to representative government. The Socratics were already aware that achievement of stable democracy depends upon historical circumstance. Attempts to specify the social conditions of democracy abound, from Aristotle to John Stuart Mill, Tocqueville, and Weber, to the many contemporary architects of the democratic theory, such as Lipset[22] and Rokkan,[23] Lerner,[24] Almond and Verba,[25] Dahl,[26] Lijphart,[27] and many other macro-historical comparative sociologists and political scientists who conduct remarkable surveys and historical studies in various parts of the world; the most recent, monumental comparative inquiry was conducted in twenty-seven developing countries of Africa, Asia, and Latin America.[28] Moreover, diversified groups of comparative social historians have been working to identify the determinants of democracy (and of such changes as development, revolution, and war) by sequence analysis conducted at various levels of causal distance. Many of them, inspired by Weber and Marx rather than by Durkheim and the functional perspective, stress various conflicts of communal interests as determining factors. Others stress, more narrowly, class conflicts, as well as conflicts between developed and undeveloped parts of the world. Most of them claim, in the words of the leading representative of this school of thought, that "[h]istory's regularities appear not in repeated sequences, replicated structures and recurrent trends on the large scale but in the causal mechanisms that link contingent sets of circumstances."[29] And they often specify those mechanisms in an original and bold manner. For instance, owing to specified sets of historical circumstances, introduction of large national armies of conscripts is claimed to have brought about political demands of the conscripts (and taxpayers) as an important determinant of the establishment of citizens' rights in many European states.[30] And, under congenial, prerevolutionary conditions, almost paradoxically, not just weakness, but also a degree of strength of the state, is claimed to have been an early prequisite for future development of democracy in much of Europe.[31]

The democratic theory builders have identified numerous near-necessary conditions for stable democracy. The conditions include: economic, especially industrial development (contingent upon development of a work ethic), emergence of the middle class as the major social stratum and of an organized working class, education, a well-established communication system, diffusion of voluntary organizations, a past development of constitutionalism, the rule of law, institutionalized political parties, and a congenial international environment. They also include legitimacy of democratic institutions, skillfulness of the society's political elite, open class structure (with only limited degree of inequality), the spread of such attitudes as trust and tolerance, and ways to accommodate group cleavages—economic, ethnic, racial, and religious. And they include the spread of the duty to respect rights and liberties of others and of "a warm and inclusive attitude toward other human beings,"[32] since, in the words of one of today's great legal defenders of liberty, a " 'free society' cannot mean one in which each individual lives in a self-centered way, without concern for his fellows' needs."[33] What all these and many other variables determine is only a probability of the successful establishment of democracy.[34] No known conjunction of the variables amounts to a sufficient condition; despite the most favorable circumstances, "a syndrome of unique historical factors" may prevent democracy from working.[35] And, even if specified (e.g., how much wealth, how much education), none of these variables is a necessary condition. "The American Revolution established a representative government in a preindustrial society, while India's democratic institutions have survived widespread poverty, illiteracy, persistent religious cleavages, and rigid class structure. Thus, given the multivariate nature of whatever causal nexus is suggested, it is inevitable that any given variable or policy will be associated with contradictory outcomes."[36]

Nonetheless, with respect to some societies, this limited knowledge can provide a reasonably safe ground for diagnosis. There are despotic systems where most near-necessary conditions of democracy are clearly present. And there are, on the other end of the spectrum, societies whose level of development makes nearly all these conditions obviously absent. This latter end of the spectrum illuminates the general problem of conditions precluding implementation of political and civil rights, and, thus, their worldwide incorporation.

However, the problem is even more pronounced within the area of social and economic rights, that is, new kinds of rights claimed as human. Our century brought a major extension of those new kinds. This extension is understandable. In its classical articulation during the Enlightenment, the human rights doctrine emerged in response to a single issue perceived as a particularly painful social problem—the suffering produced by governmental despotism. But then new social problems, that is, new socially induced kinds of major suffering, have been emerging in scores and precipitating new needs and demands, especially on the part of those who suffer.

This emergence of new social problems was due to social changes more rapid than ever before. One major reason for the rapidity has been the accelerating technological progress which has brought a continuing rise of industrial production, particularly in Europe and North America. This generated, especially in the nineteenth century, major inequalities, widespread misery, and the horrors of unemployment due to vagaries of the business cycle; a century later, following the emergence of developed industrial states, intersocietal inequalities have exceeded the intrasocietal ones. Moreover, the growth of technology, unaccompanied by implementation of adaptive policies, has brought dangerous imbalances, ranging from overpopulation to degenerative changes in the natural habitat. And, since technology can be applied for whatever use, its growth has also led, in particular in our century, to various knowingly produced disasters. First, by providing modern weapons and sophisticated systems of infiltrating and atomizing human groups, technology has facilitated the emergence and survival of new kinds of tyrannies, not only cruel, but exceptionally efficient in cruelty; the individual, especially the "different" individual belonging to various sorts of minorities, became the victim. Secondly, new technology made modern wars particularly destructive. All this means an unprecedented amount of social problems which, in turn, precipitate new and forceful demands. And many of those demands have been perceived as important enough to be articulated as rights due to any human being.

Various historical events of this century served as catalysts in this articulation, and the Second World War was most critical among them. In 1948, a long list of human rights was announced by the Universal Declaration of Human Rights. The declaration was followed, in the upcoming decades, by many international agreements, most conspicuously, the U.N. Covenant on Civil and Political Rights, and the U.N. Covenant on Economic, Social and Cultural Rights.

By ratifying these agreements, the participating states did a number of things. First, they proclaimed acceptance of political human rights as traditionally understood. Second, they added a few political and civil rights to the list, and specified some of the old ones in a new manner.[37] But the most sweeping extension of the catalog brought about by these covenants came from the inclusion of social and economic (and cultural[38]) rights, that is, broadly speaking, rights providing for greater socioeconomic equality and universal well-being. Clearly, this category of rights had rarely been claimed as "human" before.[39] Whereas for two centuries human rights served as a shield to protect the individual from activities of the state, the new category demands an ongoing state intervention for the economic and social well-being of all.

Today, there is a tendency to treat both categories—the political and civil as well as the social and economic—increasingly alike. Industrial growth generated forceful determinants of this new status of social and economic rights. One of the determinants was Marxist ideology, and another one—various kinds of non-Marxist socialism. They partially converged with liberal and leftist Christian social thought; also various antisocialist governments have been developing major components of the universal social welfare, either just for the welfare's sake or to pre-empt the socialist political claims.[40] In America of the 1930s, the ideol-ogy of the Roosevelt Revolution brought about implementation of such socioeconomic means as old age, disability and unemployment insur-ance, public housing, protection of organized labor, and protection of the worker from the established practices which deserved, in civil law language, the name of "abuse of right" of property by the employer.[41] In this manner, the United States made, in less than a decade, momentous steps toward becoming an interventionist welfare state. In addition, since the 1940s, a new kind of support for the universally "human" percep-tion of social and economic rights was coming from the Soviet Union. At face value it appeared to match the Marxist ideology which was claimed to underlie the Soviet sytem. In fact it was used as a political implement to compete with, and thus to undermine, the ideology of liberal democracies. Their political liberties and their democracy were to be replaced by the "true liberty," that is, liberty from economic want and class exploitation, and by the "true democracy" of socioeconomic equality. Since at that time the actual qualities of the Soviet system were largely unknown to the outside world, these claims, partially converg-ing with various kinds of bona fide socialist demands, had considerable impact on international opinion. No wonder, following the catalytic events of 1939–45, a substantial number of social and economic claims has been added to the list of the rights claimed human.

The Universal Declaration of Human Rights and the international agreements stipulated in its wake served as major vehicles for this addi-tion. Thus, the Declaration proclaimed everyone's entitlement to social security and to the economic, social, and cultural rights indispensable for the free development of one's personality. In particular, everyone has the right to a standard of living adequate for the health and well-being of oneself and of one's family, including food, clothing, housing, medical care, and necessary social services, and the right to security in the event of unemployment, sickness, disability, widowhood, or old age; motherhood and childhood are entitled to special care and assistance. Everyone has the right to work, to free choice of employment, to just and favorable conditions of work and remuneration, and to rest and lei-sure, including periodic holidays with pay. Everone has the right to edu-cation, and the right to freely participate in the cultural life of the community, to enjoy the arts and to share in scientific advancement. Furthermore, the Declaration pronounced various borderline rights which were, at the same time, socioeconomic and political; for instance, it proclaimed that everyone has the right to marry and found a family and to form and join trade unions.[42] The subsequent international agreements endorsed and specified many of these stipulations.

If we were to sum up all the social and economic rights claimed human by this or another group or covenant, and accept them as a part of the catalog of human rights, the catalog would be very long. Should this part be approved as a springboard for human rights policies or should the catalog be restricted to a limited number of items? This is a truly controversial question. The critics of the ongoing human rights explosion challenge both the logic and the utility of the ever-growing list, and much of their criticism refers to the fact that many of those rights are out of reach in a number of societies. They claim that "in our times 'rights' proliferate... with extraordinary speed [and] no constraints except those of the mind and appetite of their authors."[43] Claimed in large numbers and without regard to their feasibility, they often become trivial and utopian. In particular, it would be utopian to endow members of all human societies, including those at the earliest level of economic development, with such rights as "right to work, to free choice of employment, to just and favorable conditions of work and remuneration, and to rest and leisure, including periodic holidays with pay."[44] The last item has been perceived by critics as particularly ludicrous: "For millions of people who live in those parts of Asia, Africa, and South America where industrialization has hardly begun, such claims are vain and idle."[45] Consequently, add some of the critics, the "philosophically respectable concept of human rights has been muddled, obscured and debilitated," and, most importantly, the proliferation "hinders the effective protection of what are correctly seen as human rights,"[46] and brings "transvaluation of a venerable political idea: the idea of tyranny."[47]

For these reasons, some critics of the human rights explosion, even if otherwise appreciative of socioeconomic needs and demands, suggest limitation of human rights to the traditional, eighteenth-century political claims against governmental oppression.[48] Others are not that restrictive, but suggest a historical approach to the construction of the catalog: any society's historical circumstance, in particular its level of development, determines what is feasible—which of the socioeconomic, as well as political human rights can be implemented, and how to handle those which cannot be.[49]

Both demands have been challenged, and the former one has been challenged forcefully. No wonder. Dying from starvation can be perceived to be as cruel as loss of life due to political abuse, and shortage of food more painful than shortage of liberty. And extreme poverty, especially if the government is able to prevent it (and if it occurs next door to extreme wealth), easily arouses the widespread perception of the unmet claims of the poor as significant enough to be claimed human. That is why, objections notwithstanding, we face, among human rights proponents, the rising tendency to include at least some social and economic rights in the catalog. This tendency brings many of the proponents to a limited demand—the demand of incorporation determined selectively by any society's historical circumstance, that is, the incorporation of only those human rights for which social conditions already exist.

Needless to say, this selective demand brings about reservations. It suffers from a peculiar paradox. On the one hand, human rights are universally human, that is, identically due any human person, any place and at any time. On the other hand, however, for members of a social group, to be holders of a human right assumes the level of development of the group enabling them to exercise that right; otherwise, the impossible would be claimed. Does not acceptance of this historical limitation run against the equal universality of human rights? And are not those who live in undeveloped societies, by not being entitled to each and every right claimed as human, treated as if they were less human than members of more advanced nations?

The resolution of this problem seems possible, and finds a degree of support in some developments within international law. From the standpoint of their historical feasibility, the rights claimed as human can be roughly divided into two categories. First, there is among them a limited number of indispensable rights that are universally feasible today— in our era, the historical prerequisites for their implementation are present in any nation, irrespective of its level of development. There are here such claims as the right against torture, genocide, racial discrimination, and slave trade. Today, every government is able to respect these rights. They are now so widely perceived as "inalienable" and "inherently human," that they become increasingly recognized as rights *iuris cogentis*, that is, rights imposed on all nations, irrespective of any nation's acquiescence, by peremptory norms of customary international law; these rights may not be set aside by provisions of a treaty, and anyone who breaks them becomes "*hostis humani generis,* an enemy of all mankind."[50] Clearly, this category of rights is actually, and not only potentially universally human.

However, the majority of the rights claimed as human are, at least as yet, not of this kind; the majority can be immediately implemented in some, but not in other societies. Democracy, right to unemployment benefits, rest and leisure, and sharing in scientific advancement are among them. Each of them is clearly feasible in the most advanced societies, clearly unfeasible in societies at the opposite end of the developmental scale, and each hangs in a somewhat nebulous area in societies at the intermediate level of development. Thus, they are potentially rather than actually universal or, in other words, "relative and progressive" rather than "absolute and immediate."[51] This is, as indicated earlier, particularly true of the right to democracy: when the authors of the Universal Declaration proclaimed that "[e]veryone has the right to take part in the Government of his country, directly or through freely chosen representatives" (art. 21/1), they had in mind, as asserted in the Preamble, "a common standard of achievement for all peoples and all nations, to the end that every individual and every organ of society...shall strive," rather than an immediate right in all societies. And even today, in spite of the growing number of signatories of the U.N. Covenant on Civil and Political Rights (which articulates, in article 25, the right to democracy in categorical manner[52]), this right can hardly be perceived as absolute and immediate; it may be immediately claimed only in societies where its prerequisites are in place.

The very admission of this historical limitation of human rights is disappointing. Moreover, it is dangerous; it can easily be abused. Any autocrat can always insist that his society, whatever its level of development, or some of its categorically selected groups, are not yet ready for the exercise of various human rights, especially the right to representative government; it may be difficult to rebut this argument, however self-serving it might be. And if the political powerholders in a society on a genuinely low level of development use this argument, they cannot be expected to willingly promote conditions for democracy and other human rights, and thus pave the way for the abolition of their own privilege.

Here, however, at least some legal remedies are at hand. To be sure, they are difficult. One of them is hermeneutical; implied by the familiar demand of "taking rights seriously," it consists in acceptance of an important device: when in doubt, a society's readiness for the implementation of any human right is to be presumed.[53] The second remedy is more complex and requires some lawmaking: whenever, owing to the level of development of a society, the presumption of readiness can be rebutted by its government, the rights that cannot be implemented immediately should bring about the government's obligation to build social and economic prerequisites for their implementation. This can only be accomplished by an energetic and, at the same time, reasonable pursuit of cultural and economic development.[54] This obligation was implied by article 28 of the Universal Declaration of Human Rights: "Everyone is entitled to a social...order in which the rights and freedoms set forth in this Declaration can be fully realized." It was implied by the preamble to the Declaration: the rights declared are "a common standard of achievement...to the end that every organ of society...shall strive by teaching and education to promote respect for these rights...and by progressive measures...to secure their universal and effective recognition and observance." And it became a part of article 2 of the U.N. Covenant on Economic, Social, and Cultural Rights: "Each State Party...undertakes to take steps...to the maximum of its available resources, with a view to achieving progressively the full realization of the rights recognized by the present Covenant by all appropriate means."

These provisions pave the way for new instruments of international law, establishing, for every undeveloped society, the right to development as a condition for human rights incorporation, that is, a right subservient to human rights. This would be a right benefitting a people rather than a human right. It would be an international right directed against the government of the society to be developed. And it can feasibly be established by international *pacta in favorem tertii*—agreements among states to energetically press authoritarian governments to pursue development of their populations. Once a right of this kind is estalished in international law, foreign states and international organizations would be able to exercise pressure against any government reluctant to fulfill the corresponding obligations; which would prevent the future Bokassas, Noriegas, Mengistus or Ceausescus not only from malicious disregard of their nation's need for develpoment, but also from bringing about the nation's economic and cultural regression and ruin.[55] This should provide at least an important step towards the eventual resolution of the problem of historical conditions hindering the process of incorporation.

To be sure, however important, this would be a partial remedy only. Most preindustrial societies (as well as ravaged societies) are unable to effectively pursue developmental policies without helpful cooperation, in particular, without economic and technological assistance and capital investment coming from the outside world. No wonder demands for such helpful cooperation abound.[56] However, there are unprecedented economic, political, demographic and environmental upheavals in the world today. They have been generated, among other things, by the sequence of the long-lasting economic burden of the cold war followed by the sudden end of the cold war economy, by the side effects of the ongoing new industrial revolution, and by technology increasingly outdistancing culture. Because of the upheavals, the help coming from the outside world is disturbingly scarce in comparison with the needs caused by the plight of most developing societies. The scarcity hampers (and often reverses) development. The developmental setbacks are responsible for continuing widespread misery; and, particularly important for this writing, they constitute today a major difficulty in providing conditions for human rights' worldwide incorporation: "Increases in malnutrition, infant mortality, unemployment, social pathologies, environmental degradation and forced migration are facts that make a mockery of the legal commitments [in the covenants] to achieve progressively the fulfillment of the rights set forth."[57]

Incorporation and Problems with International Law

Other difficulties with incorporation come from the major problems plaguing international law itself. International law is a decentralized system. "Domestic law can be imposed by...the officials of the state. [But, in the] international society, composed of sovereign states... no...central lawgiving and law-enforcing authority" exists.[58] Consequently, the whole of international law, by being loosely structured, remains an undeveloped legal system. In particular, international law suffers from a confusing variety of ill-defined sources. It also lacks an efficient mechanism of enforcement. And these two predicaments have been especially acute in the area of international law of human rights, since the area constitutes a relatively new and immature set of norms. I will start with the novelty of the international law of human rights, and then turn to the broader problems of its ill-defined sources and inefficiency of enforcement.

Human rights as a new area of international law. Until this century, it had been a dominant dogma of international law that the way a sovereign government treats its citizens is solely its own business. Accordingly, foreign governments and other groups had no title to interfere in the event of mistreatment. And even more so, since only states, not individuals, had been subjects of international law, it was unthinkable to demand that mistreated individuals be given, by international law, the right to challenge their own government in domestic courts. This noninterference served the interests of sovereign governments; whereas most governments were concerned about mutual compliance of states with accepted norms of trade or of peace and war, they rarely cared what another state did to its subjects, and, reciprocally, they did not want their own behavior to be scrutinized. It was only in this century, and especially in the wake of World War II, that the doctrine of noninterference began to crumble, and international human rights law was born.

To be sure, there had been predecessors, some of them as distant and feeble as *iuris gentium* remedies in Rome and claims for religious tolerance in the Middle Ages. In modern times, there were "humanitarian interventions" organized by states or groups of states to protect minorities abroad from abuse and massacre which, like the slaughter of the Maronites in Lebanon in 1860 and the Armenians in Turkey between 1890 and 1919, were claimed to have "shocked the conscience of mankind." There were also occasional, specialized treaties dealing with human rights, such as the minority treaties of Berlin in 1878 and of Versailles in 1919, as well as the pathbreaking labor conventions, a few of them preceding, and many more following establishment of the International Labor Organization in 1919. However it was only over the last fifty years that the system of law of international human rights started to emerge—a system still in the making and far from maturation.

Owing to its unparalleled cruelties, miseries, and hopes, World War II stimulated a strong desire for a better world and, largely under American influence, a renaissance of the human rights idea; suddenly, in the wake of committed atrocities, it became clearer that the way any government treated its subjects was no longer solely its own business. This notion did at least partially illuminate Roosevelt's Four Freedoms pronouncement, the provisions of the Atlantic Charter, and the Charter of the United Nations with its recognition of "respect for human rights and fundamental freedoms for all without distinction as to race, sex, language, or religion."[59] The Universal Declaration of Human Rights, adopted in 1948 was followed in subsequent decades by many international agreements. They included the two U.N. covenants, on political and on socioeconomic rights. There were also regional treaties, and a number of other, more specialized instruments, directed against such wrongs as genocide, cruelties of criminal procedure, and various kinds of discrimination, especially racial, religious, and sex discrimination. These agreements have been perceived as sources of the newly emerging part of international law.

The problem with the sources of international law. However, the whole of international law is of intolerably loose structure. The most important reason for this is the peculiar character of its sources. In contrast with the domestic laws of nation states, norms of international law are not enacted by a central organ, such as a formally established legislative body. Instead, a number of other sources exist, and their hierarchy is not always clear. A list of these sources has been registered by article 38 of the Statute of the International Court of Justice. International custom and international treaties, traditionally perceived as the two main sources, open the list. Since international law is largely customary law, international custom has always been a source of major importance. The custom becomes customary law if it amounts to general and long-lasting practice (*diuturnus usus*) exercised by the states in the conviction that its exercise is legally binding (*opinio iuris*).

However important, the custom is, as a source of law, vaguely defined and often hard to prove. In particular, it is difficult to specify which organs of the states are supposed to exercise the practice, how uniform must the practice be, and how explicit must its acceptance as law be in order to transform a lasting custom into customary law. These questions have long been contested by international lawyers. For instance, on the last issue, some claim that *diuturnus usus* itself, especially if exercised without protest, provides sufficient assumption of *opinio iuris*, whereas others demand independent admission on the part of the states that the *opinio* is there; the admission may be contained in such declarations as international treaties, executive decisions, pronouncements of lawmakers, courts, and respected jurists.[60]

International treaties constitute another source.[61] To be sure, only some of them do. Most international treaties, especially agreements between a few states, if intended to be terminated once the duties of the parties have been performed, bind only the parties involved; they impose obligations on the parties on the ground of a higher level principle that promises should be kept.[62] Thus, those treaties are not, per se, a source of law; they generate solely contractual obligations. Only if these contractual obligations become consistently accepted in the practice of states (and organizations) other than the parties, and the acceptance occurs in the belief that they are legally binding, does the treaty become a source of customary international law.

On the other hand, the "law-making" international treaties are an independent source of international law; that is, they are a source independent of custom. Their widespread emergence is a modern development. They are multilateral agreements creating sets of general norms addressed not just to the original parties, but also explicitly open for future access by all states of the world or of a major region. Their law-making effect is "at least as great as the general practice considered sufficient to support a customary rule"[63]; thus, if the conclusion of any of them produces norms intentionally contradicting the customary law in force, the new norms replace the customary ones. But this independence of the new norms from custom is not absolute; the new norms may be subsequently reshaped by customary changes, and even lose their validity through desuetude. The rise of the law-making treaties has been dramatic in our century—so much so that they have been gaining "paramouncy over customary international law. The treaty-making process is a rational and orderly one, permitting participation in the creation of law by all States on a basis of equality," including the newly independent states.[64]

But, whatever the advantages of the treaties over custom, both are imperfect as sources of law: the system of norms produced by them is full of ambiguities, inconsistencies, and, consequently, contradictions. This is obviously due to the characteristics of customary law. However, it is also due to problems with the "law-making" treaties themselves—those treaties constitute only a distant analogy to the orderly domestic legislative process. The "law-making" treaties are numerous.[65] Most of them are uneasy compromises reflecting a variety of conflicting interests and ideologies. They are negotiated, drafted, and adopted under the auspices of many international organizations—universal and regional, general and specialized. This "dispersal of law-making activities gives rise to...inconsistent and mutually incompatible [treaties] which may overlap...or...fail to address subjects that merit regulation. [And,] since the differences among the norms contained in various human rights instruments are numerous, the potential for conflicts is virtually unlimited.... Conflicts also arise among instruments adopted within the same organization, and even among various provisions of the same instruments."[66]

Conflicts of norms, that is, conflicts of rights and duties, bedevil moral and legal systems. Owing, in particular, to the stimulating force of rights, they are dangerous. They undermine operation of social institutions, especially economic and political, and tend to produce, in domestic and international relations, "anger, revenge and annihilation;" hence, the basic need for uniformity.[67] This need is being met by nation-states of today by the means of a few specific steps. The first of them is development of legal norms articulated with precision and clustered in coordinated systems; this can be done with a high degree of efficiency by the legislative branch of modern governments. But even the optimal degree of legislative precision does not amount to perfect precision. Legal norms are comprised of unavoidably ambiguous terms, and the ambiguity always leaves room for conflicts of norms. The ambiguity begs for binding interpretation, and the interpretation is most often provided by courts, especially the highest courts of appeals;[68] in this manner—through skillful lawmaking and judicial interpretation—the need for uniformity is largely met by developed legal systems.

This method, however, has never been widely open to international law. First, as I just noted, "law-making" treaties are a far cry from skillful legislative activity. And, second, there is no international court system comparable to its national counterparts in advanced societies.[69] To be sure, some remedies have been tried to rectify the former predicament, most importantly the increasing use of "codification," that is, of multilateral treaties intended as restatement of the norms in force; preceded by early, private attempts,[70] substantial work has been done in this area, since 1949, by the United Nations International Law Commission. The "codification" brought a degree of progress in unifying some components of the system (with the 1982 Convention on the Law of the Sea as a particularly marked success). However, this has been a fragmentary progress only, and the degree of specificity and binding power of the norms thus restated can hardly be compared with those of the norms codified in advanced domestic legal systems.

To patch up the inconsistencies produced by custom and treaty, article 38 lists the "general principles of law recognized by civilized nations" as another source of international law. Its application can be perceived as filling gaps in international law by use, *per analogiam*, of fundamental and widely accepted norms of domestic legal systems. And two further, "subsidiary" sources listed by article 38—decisions of international courts and writings of outstanding jurists of various nations—have been added, in particular, to clarify ambiguities and contraditions.

However useful those further sources may be, the meaning, validity, and weight of each of them is, again, uncertain. Thus, there is widespread disagreement on what the "general principles of law recognized by civilized nations" are, and whether these principles may constitute a valid source of international law at all. The former issue was contested even among the members of the very committee of jurists who drafted the Court's Statute;[71] the latter has been answered negatively by those trying to constrain international interference into their state's activities.[72] Also the validity and degree of influence of the subsidiary sources, especially judicial decisions, is open to challenges. The application of *stare decisis*, even though narrowly accepted in the practice of the International Court of Justice, seems precluded by article 59 of its Statute,[73] and understandably so; each of the relatively few cases under its jurisdiction has so many peculiar characteristics, and some judges are so vehemently guided by political considerations and current interests of their respective nations, that particular caution is necessary before the tenuous line dividing lawmaking from adjudication may be allowed to be crossed.

Even these cursory comments should make it clear why the thus formed norms of international law are much more vague and less structured than their counterparts on the law books of modern states. In particular, it is more difficult to specify the meaning of these norms, their process of change is often unclear, their legal validity controversial (especially due to the way in which custom turns into customary law), and their system is full of contradictions and particularly wide gaps leaving room for a high rate of unprovided cases. No wonder, complaints abound that international law is acutely unclear on what behavior is demanded and, especially, prohibited. Which brings about the ultimate question: "how can international law claim to be a system of restraint if it lacks a means to identify transgressions?"[74]

The problem of enforcement. The inefficiency of enforcement mechanism is another major problem with international law; as I just noted, there is no central authority to enforce international law. Accordingly, "[t]o many an observer, governments seem largely free to decide whether to agree to new law [and] whether to comply with agreed law. International law, then, is voluntary and only hortatory. It must always yield to national interest.... Indeed, some lawyers seem to despair for international law until there is world government or at least effective international organization."[75]

What are the existing international law enforcement mechanisms? In want of well-organized central organs, international law resorts to a number of dispersed implements. The traditional ones include unilateral use of force in response to aggression, various kinds of nonmilitary retaliation for violations, especially, termination of economic or diplomatic relations, denial of reciprocation in response to infringement of a reciprocal relationship, as well as efforts to publicly censure the law-breaking state. This century brought an addition of further important devices. One of them is a new way of organizing sanctions against those states that threaten peace or start a war. In particular, following the more limited steps of the League of Nations covenant, the United Nations Charter proclaims the Security Council's power to impose economic sanctions, to interrupt communications and to severe diplomatic relations with a state that commits aggression, and, ultimately, to apply the force of arms.[76] This sounds like an establishment of a central organ capable of compelling compliance. However, owing to deep divisions within the international community and the veto power of the Council's permanent members, the sanctions can be applied only in those rare cases when not only the majority of the Council, but all its permanent members as well, find the sanctions politically expedient.

Another major development of this century, aimed not only at infringements of peace, but also at other kinds of violations, is the emergence of international courts, in particular, of the Permanent Court of International Justice established in 1922, and replaced, since 1945, by the International Court of Justice.[77] Their prestige has been marked; when the International Court of Justice, its jurisdiction duly established, pronounces a decision, noncompliance is difficult. International courts grew out of arbitral tribunals—the tribunals known since the 1794 Jay Treaty and widespread today, comprised of arbiters appointed by the parties for the settlement of a specific dispute or class of disputes. Originally, arbitral tribunals were often asked for judgments *ex aequo et bono*— based on fairness and goodness—but since the end of the nineteenth century these tribunals have largely turned to international law as ground for decisions. International courts differ from arbitral tribunals in some respects, in particular by the fact that the composition of the courts is basically determined in advance, on a permanent basis, by their statute (and not by an *ad hoc* agreement of the contestants), and their rules of adjudication and procedure are more rigidly defined. Nonetheless, they share an essential characteristic with the tribunals: their jurisdiction depends upon consent by the parties;[78] in this sense, they are courts of arbitration. And even those states that accept, *a priori*, wide jurisdiction of the International Court of Justice "as compulsory *ipso facto* and without special agreement,"[79] most often qualify the acceptance by reservations providing them with easy ways out;[80] thus, when a state anticipates losing an important case or being harassed by difficult litigation, the resort to reservations becomes an obvious response. This prerequisite of consent by the parties is the main reason why the jurisdiction of international courts is very limited and court settlements are exceptional among the states; in the years 1946–1988, the International Court of Justice has dealt altogether with sixty contentious cases (and twenty requests for advisory opinions).[81]

All this means weakness of enforcement: "whether...a successful ...attempt will be made to enforce international law [does not] depend primarily upon...the disinterested operation of law-enforcing mechanisms. Both attempt and success depend upon political considerations and the actual distribution of power in a particular case."[82] This weakness of enforcement has been particularly marked with respect to international law of human rights; in the decades following the Second World War, we have been witnessing largely unopposed and unsanctioned nonperformance of human rights treaties by a large proportion of their signatories (covering the majority of the world's population), from the Chinese and, until recently, the Soviets, to many other oppressive governments of the left and the right. Furthermore, when undertaking an occasional action against violators, governments have often used infringements of human rights as a convenient pretext for their own political purposes.

Some recent developments and a new promise. The preceding comments should make it clear why international law suffers from two major drawbacks—its vagueness and fragmentary structure, as well as its widespread nonenforcement. Both provide for a high degree of ineffectiveness. The ineffectiveness is (besides the developmental variation of human societies discussed earlier) the main reason why there has been a high degree of skepticism about the promise of worldwide incorporation of the international law of human rights.

But, however understandable this skepticism may be, the promise of the incorporation does not seem impossible today; some recent international developments provide a newly emerging chance. They consist in the ongoing decline of the most powerful tyrannies. The decline, if answered by well-conceived policies on the part of open societies and especially of the United States—which is a big *if* indeed—can bring about a new, agreed upon limitation of any nation's sovereignty in favor of an effective, central international organization. And this would entail a better structured system of sources, as well as more energetic enforcement of international law and, especially, of the international law of human rights.

In the wake of World War II, the United Nations was conceived as exactly this kind of international organization. The idea did not work. The growth of the Soviet Union with its dependencies, having brought about sharp division of the world, became the most important obstacle undermining the role of the United Nations. However, recently, the Soviet empire went through a spectacular moral, political, and economic decline. The empire emerged in the name of highly idealistic, historicist social philosophy which, even if well intended, proved to be a false prophecy. When dealing with human work, the philosophy contains a wrongheaded theory of motivation that prevented communist societies from building viable economies.[83] The utopian character of its philosophy, as well as its economic failure, contributed to complete ideological bankruptcy of the communist system; and so did the immense suffering caused by long-lasting efforts to make the utopia work, especially the efforts consisting in extreme concentration of unchecked political power. Today, it is possible to find substantial, even though shrinking, groups of communist believers in various Western societies, but it is difficult to find them in communist and formerly communist countries. This ideological bankruptcy has become, since the late 1980s, transparent in Eastern and Central Europe and in the Soviet Union; and, in the wake of the Tiananmen Square massacre, it became transparent in China as well. It also became clear to anyone in every communist society to what degree their political elites had turned out to be void of any ethical and social concerns; the motivation of the elites had been largely reduced to two powerful feelings—fear of their own people, and relentless greed. Subsequently, the communist states lost whatever legitimacy they might have had in the past.

It is impossible to predict the post-Soviet future, and even more so the future of China. Sovietologists have been developing lists of feasible upcoming scenarios, from impending civil war, chaos, and mass migrations; to a new wave of nationalistic militarism, fascism, xenophobia, and bigotry; to gradual transformation of both powers into more open societies, especially the transformation of the Soviet empire into an increasingly democratic federation or a group of independent and increasingly democratic nations. Clearly, some version of the last alternative would best meet the human rights concerns.

Of course, this is a difficult alternative; the problems of the transformation are exacting. Few parts of the communist world had ever known working democracy. And, wherever seeds of democracy existed, they were undermined or erased. In particular, constitutional systems or their nascent elements had been replaced by dictatorial or oligarchic concentration of political power—the power strenghtened by the unique fact that the despots had controlled virtually all of their nation's capital. Legality was gone, and, especially, judicial independence and excellence (which had been, in Russia, a particularly proud achievement in the wake of reforms under Alexander II). Not only did political parties disappear, but so did other components of civic society. In Stalinist times, communist societies became, "empty space societies,"[84] with the autocratic state at the top of the social structure, and the individual (or individual family) at the bottom, without any voluntary organizations or independent groups in between.[85] The economies have been ruined, and the work ethic largely erased by near total divorce between the worker's quality of work and wages, characteristic for the Soviet-style command economy. How to bring about the painful market-oriented structural transformation without hurting the population strongly enough to undermine the road to democracy, no one knows. In 1948, the Marshall Plan went into effect, and became a critical implement of Europe's recovery; today, the liberal democracies, undermined by a protracted economic impairment and a widespread atrophy of leadership, have been unable to provide even the amount of assistance necessary to establish a basic safety net for the crucial, preliminary period following budget balancing reforms in Russia and other postcommunist societies. And, most dangerously, major parts of these societies are torn by intense strife among sometimes intricately interspersed ethnic groups, with ethnic hatreds often nourished, especially in the Soviet past, for imperial purposes, but kept, by the power of the police state, from turning into violent outbreaks. Transformation to democracy, by removing the police state, brings about in each of the former Soviet republics and other parts of the communist world, the danger of ethnic wars. No wonder, these societies are overwhelmed by fear of the future. And the members of the old-time oppressive elite from within the comunist party, political police, and the army, acutely aware that their loss of political might may easily mean not only loss of privilege and wealth, but of life as well, can turn to arms, to defend their power. All this means that the road to democracy is rough. And, even if successful in a number of generations, it will be a difficult road, with setbacks, some of them bloody. We have already witnessed the massacres in Timsoara, Vilnius, Riga, Grozny, and Transcaucasian republics, as well as the sMoscow events of 1991 and 1993, and the list is growing.

However, from the standpoint of this writing, the future may be promising. The main concern stressed here is a more efficient central international organization and more efficient international law as an avenue for universal human rights incorporation. If, despite all odds, the transition to democracy in the former Soviet territories and dependencies continues, the United Nations (or, maybe, another international body to replace the U.N.) will be increasingly able to play its originally conceived role; international law may then become a better structured legal system with bite, and we will be on the way to gradual incorporation of human rights in Russia and its remaining peripheries. If, on the other hand, Russia and other post-Soviet states do not succeed and go through a period of major upheavals, their chance of social and economic recovery will probably dwindle, and their military power will further decline. If left alone by the outside world, their ruling elites may still be able to oppress their populations for some time. But, again, granted that the open societies respond to upheavals by well conceived policies, the conjunction of internal and external pressures can bring about general progress in incorporating human rights into an increasing number of domestic laws of various nations in and out of the former Soviet spheres of influence. Whether China will follow suit at that or, feasibly, at an earlier, more congenial stage, and under what circumstances, no one can predict. Thus, whatever the future developments within the post-communist societies—their democratic growth or their authoritarian decline—there seems to be a chance of the eventual universal incorporation, that is, of the human rights becoming legal rights persistently implemented throughout the globe.

If and when this occurs, the incorporation will consist in enactment and enforcement of human rights by all domestic legal systems. This enactment would produce national, internally consistent catalogs of human rights. The catalogs, despite a universal common core, would vary, due to diverse levels of development; but, in the course of growth of the less developed areas, the catalogs would increasingly tend toward a greater degree of global uniformity. For enforcement, a battery of domestic means registered earlier will have to be used.[86]

If this triumph of universal incorporation arrives, its arrival will be a legal product of the ongoing moral struggle, that is, of the impact of human rights experiences on all domestic legal systems. Moreover, an important effect in the opposite direction should also occur; in feedback, the legal implementation cannot but reinforce human rights experiences throughout the world. Both processes would amount to the achievement of a high degre of moral and political unity of all members of the human species.

But would this achievement be irreversible, and thus support the conclusion that the struggle for human rights is over? Since we acquire moral experiences, and human rights experiences among them, in the process of social learning, this conclusion might be acceptable if environmental changes produced structural changes in us, and if we passed them on our descendants. However, this is not the case. Lamarck was wrong; we do not inherit learned characteristics and, subsequently, no human child will ever be born with a programmed dedication to human rights experiences.[87] Accordingly, every child in every new generation will have to be taught such experiences from scratch. And since new problems facing future generations cannot be anticipated, this process may encounter unpredictable difficulties and moral as well as legal setbacks. That is why, the triumph of incorporation notwithstanding, each generation will have to continue the struggle, and—in a loose paraphrase of Heraclitus' words—may have to fight for the rights "as for the walls of the city."[88] Which provides us with still another difficulty of human rights struggle, in this case an everlasting one. And all the impediments registered here bring us squarely to our original and conclusive issue— to the importance of justification.

Notes

1. The research on these and other controversies among cognitive developmental psychologists has been unusually rich, and a wealth of empirical reports and of analytical studies has been published. A number of earlier and recent reviews of this literature include, in particular: Hoffman 1970, 1977; Rest 1984; Darley and Shultz 1990; Garrod 1993.
2. See, in particular, Piaget 1932; Kohlberg 1981, 1984.
3. Despite the name "cognitive-developmental psychology," I stress here both the emotional and cognitive devolopment, thus avoiding Piaget's cognitive onesidedness and coming closer to Kohlberg's more balanced approach. My reason for this should be clear in view of the understanding of morality accepted in the introduction to this book: moral experiences, having emotive, driving character, are not a part of cognition, and that is why they require a necessary degree of emotional maturity in the first place; on the other hand, as exemplified in the several upcoming lines of this text, their emergence also depends on the development of cognitive skills.
4. Those are the facts the statements of which serve, in a developed moral system, as small premises in normative deductions, see 19-20, *supra.*
5. The capacity to comprehend these facts, especially by emotional-cognitive empathy, has been stressed, in particular, by Piaget and Kohlberg (influenced, in turn, by G.H. Mead); they consider the experience of social participation and of role-taking as prerequisites for the acquisition of the capacity. For a recent rearticulation of the development of empathic distress in children and young adults, and of its impact on activation of such moral principles as benevolence, equality and equity, see Hoffman 1993.
6. Cf. 6, *supra.*
7. Cf. Gorecki 1979: 17-18.
8. *Ibid.,* 17-27.

9. For many other instances, see Ossowska 1971: 27-97. All these instances do not imply a conscious translation of interests or needs into practical prescriptions— such translation would provide an instrumental rather than the moral motivation.

10. The selectiveness occurs often in bad faith. However, this is not always the case. *Bona fide* selectiveness is feasible; governments sometimes sacrifice a human right in good faith (for instance, on utilitarian grounds considered overriding) to protect other values or rights, including rights sheltering political interests.

11. The Preamble to the Declaration.

12. Lauterpacht 1950: 397.

13. For example, the declaration condemning slave trade of blacks, at the Vienna Convention of 1815, became the early stepping stone for later developments culminating in its abolition (Nahlik 1967: 104-5). And, in the post-Stalinist decades, the more daring members of the legal profession in some parts of Eastern and Central Europe were fighting for full implementation of citizens' rights as spelled out on the law books, especially the rights of criminal defendants which, even though formally promulgated, had been widely denied until the mid-1950s. This struggle turned, in Poland of the 1970s, into a well-organized defense of striking workers and dissidents by the antigovernmental Workers' Defense Committee— a group whose activity became particularly instrumental in the emergence of Solidarity in 1980.

14. This perception has been accepted by human rights advocates on different grounds. Today, the majority of them consider international human rights law as higher level positive law, not just "beyond," but also "above" the nations (Cf., e.g., Henkin 1978: 89ff). But, in reaction against the near-uniformly positivistic fashion of the last, and of the early part of our century, there has also been some return to the idea of natural law as a higher-level system, and natural human rights as a part of it. When analyzing an opinion of the International Court of Justice (in the case of Reservations to the Convention on the Prevention and Punishment of the Crime of Genocide, [1951] ICJ Reports 23), Judge Tanaka found the "seat of human rights...not in any positive law...but in 'the conscience of mankind' and 'moral law,' which are nothing else but natural law. In regard to such matters authorities of any state play only a declaratory role" (Tanaka 1972: 254).

15. "Incorporation" is understood here broadly enough to fit either monist or dualist perception of international vs. domestic law, and this enables us to avoid entanglement in the "monism-dualism" debate. Dualists treat international law and domestic law of any nation-state as two separate systems; thus, to become a part of the domestic order, norms of international law which pronounce human rights must be incorporated, by lawmakers, into domestic law. On the other hand, monists treat international and domestic law as a single system; within that system, international law is percieved (at least by such monists as Hans Kelsen or Alfred Verdross) as a set of higher level norms enforceable *ipso iure* by domestic courts and agencies. However, no domestic law will ever enforce *ipso iure* norms of international law without an overriding domestic norm, most often constitutional, ordering the *ipso iure* enforcement.

16. The disclaimers come from some pragmatically oriented defenders of moral idealism. For instance, in Nicholas Rescher's words, "[h]aving and pursuing an ideal, regardless of its impracticability, can yield benefits such as a better life for ourselves and a better world for our posterity.... As Max Weber observed...even in the domain of politics, which has been called the 'art of the possible,' the possible has frequently been attained only through striving for something impos-

sible that lies beyond one's reach" (Rescher 1987: 137). Whatever the degree of validity of this important moral stand, it would be difficult to accept it as a basis for lawmaking (cf. ch. 5, n. 18, *infra*).

17. Those agreements include the U.N. Declaration on the Right to Development, U.N. Declaration on the Right of Peoples to Peace, Articles 21-24 of the African Charter on Human and Peoples' Rights, some norms of the U.N. Covenants on Civil and Political Rights (Articles 1 and 47) and on Economic, Social and Cultural Rights (Articles 1 and 25), as well as the (explicitly recommendatory) General Assembly Resolution on Permanent Sovereignty over Natural Resources.

18. "[A]s policy goals, as standards of morality [these claims] would be acceptable and one could...agree on practical programmes for attaining these good ends. [However,] to give the new rights an actual legal context...is the casual introduction of serious confusions of thought (Brownlie 1988: 14-15).

19. Pressure for this inclusion has been exerted, in particular, by international lawyers and politicians from various new African and Asian states. For them, the inclusion of collective rights to self-determination or to free use of natural resources pertains to the struggle for decolonization, and inclusion of the right to development—to the struggle to overcome the inherited poverty. Consequently, they consider collective rights to be of such essential importance that, to be better protected, those rights should, in their view, be codified as "human." On the other hand they are less concerned with traditional, political human rights. In their societies, where individualism is an alien philosophy, the notion of the individual all but disappears in favor of the roles ascribed to everyone in the all-important collectivity; which makes for them "the idea that people would possess a non-community-linked human identity...absolutely inconceivable" (VanderWal 1990: 83); VanderWal refers here to such writers as Eddison Zvobogo and Asmarom Legesse, as well as Keba Mbaye—the Senegalese jurist who launched, in 1972, the idea of "human right to development." Many critics of this stand admit the importance of collective rights as moral rights, and also as legal rights, especially *de lege ferenda*. However, the critics challenge the *human* character of those rights forcefully. First, since human rights are, *ex definitione*, rights of the human individual, "human rights of collectivities," if not reducible to individual claims against the state (as, for instance, right to freedom of assembly, to representative government, or rights of minorities—where every individual belonging to the group is the right-holder), constitute a self-contradiction, and thus blur the human rights idea badly. This is not just a semantic issue: "Human rights are a rare and valuable intellectual and moral resource in the struggle to right the balance between society (and state) and the individual. Unless we preserve their distinctive character, including standing firm on their character as individual rights, their positive role in the struggle for human dignity will be seriously, perhaps even fatally, compromised" (Donnelly 1989: 149; 1990: 49). Moreover, the practical implications of "collective human rights" are dangerous: whose rights are they, and whose obligations do they imply? In particular, are they rights of unstructured general populations against their own state (or other countries, or the world at large), or are they rights of the state exercised "in care" of its people? Since the latter is often the case, "the so-called human rights of states [easily turn] against the human rights of individual citizens, transforming human rights from an instrument of human liberation into a new and particularly cruel cloack for repression"(Donnelly 1990: 47). Collective human right to development is believed to make this danger particularly marked; armed with this right, "[i]mpatient governments will...be

tempted to impose their...policies on their recalcitrant populations by a variety of means [including] press censorship, the direction of labour, and the prohibition of trade union activities...and unfortunately such measures are only too often apt to lead eventually to the forceful suppression of all dissent, and to end with re-education camps, 'disappearances,' and firing-squads" (Sieghart 1985: 166). And, on the top of that, the inclusion of the collective right to development into the catalog of human rights is not helpful in promoting the development itself (see ch. 5, n. 56, *infra*).

20. Gellhorn 1960: 163.
21. This wording, used especially in the international law of human rights, divides political rights into political rights in stricter sense (that is rights to political par-ticipation) and civil rights (that is rights to other lieberties of the citizen). On another, uniquely American meaning of "civil rights" (and "civil rights legisla-tion"), see the text to the preceding note.
22. In particular Lipset 1959, [1960] 1981, 1994.
23. Lipset and Rokkan 1967; Rokkan 1970.
24. Lerner 1958.
25. Almond and Verba 1963.
26. Dahl 1971.
27. Lijphart 1977, 1984.
28. Diamond, Linz and Lipset 1988-89.
29. Tilly 1993: 18.
30. Tilly, 1990 and 1993, *passim* . For an interesting, similar but prospectivie view of the Soviet armed forces expressed at the end of the last decade, see Shtromas, 1988: 260-71.
31. Tilly 1993, *passim*. Cf. also Adam Ulam's words dealing with the current circum-stance in Russia and Ukraine: "Why have the Russian and Ukrainian economies declined so disastrously in the last five years? Mostly because of the collapse of political authority, first in the USSR and then in its two main legatees. What is necessary for real economic reform to be effective and acceptable to the people? Alas, mainly a strong and centralized political authority. Of course, there are obvious dangers to the latter, but the continuation of present political turbulence poses a much greater danger" (Ulam 1994: 41).
32. Almond and Verba (1963: 11), referring to Harold Lasswell's personality charac-teristics of the "democrat."
33. Gellhorn 1960: 169.
34. The discoveries of the democratic theory, as well as the general, common sense observation of the world around, have had a major intellectual impact. In particu-lar, the idea of citizenship—qualities, attitudes, and responsibilities of citizens— as an historical determinant of emergence and survival of liberal democracy, became, in the last decade, a widely debated subject of political philosophy; for a recent survey see Kymlicka and Norman 1994. Interestingly, the survey starts with an account of Rawls' partial revision of his earlier monumental work, limit-ing the feasibility of his project to societies where civic culture had taken hold (Rawls 1993).
35. Lipset 1981: 28.
36. Lipset 1994: 17.
37. For instance, the Universal Declaration of Human Rights pronounces everybody's right to be free from "attacks upon his honor and reputation" (art. 12), "to leave any country, including his own, and to return to his country" (art.13), and to

"asylum from persecution" (art. 14). And other covenants stipulated in the wake of the Universal Declaration add such items as the right to name or to nationality (art.24 of the U.N. Covenant on Civil and Political Rights, and arts.18 and 20 of the American Convention on Human Rights), or rights of members of minorities (art.27 of the U.N. Covenant on Civil and Political Rights).

38. Cultural rights are of importance and interest, but I treat them paranthetically here, since in a society where political and socioeconomic rights are protected, whatever is understood as "cultural rights" of a human individual (and not of a people) is, at least basically, protected as well. This is particularly true, under article 27 of the International Covenant on Civil and Political Rights, of the right "to enjoy their own culture" by members of minority groups. (On the other hand, the peoples' cultural rights, especially the peoples' right to self-determination, constitute a difficult area; from Canada to various parts of the former Soviet Union to many other countries of the world, it is unclear and controversial what does "a people" mean and how far should its self-determination go.)

39. To be sure, sometimes it was, at least implicitly. For instance, the short-lived French Constitution of 1791 provided for public aid for the poor and free public education, and John Stuart Mill displayed not only concern about social justice and general welfare, but socialist sympathies as well. However, basically, equal political liberty rather than economic equality or welfare for all had been the notion underlying the idea of human rights since its articulation in the eighteenth century.

40. Bismarck's policies are a well-known instance here.

41. These practices, including absence of maximum working hours, use of child labor, and absence of minimum wages, had been, in the preceding decades, largely sheltered by the Supreme Court in numerous decisions, with *Lochner v. New York* (198 U.S. 45 [1905]), *Hammer v. Dagenhart* (247 U.S. 251 [1918]), and *Adkins v. Children's Hospital* (261 U.S. 525 [1923]) among those most pronounced. Sheltering of these practices provides an instance of how the ideology of rights can be used (and abused) by powerful interest groups to protect extremes of callousness and greed.

42. This list comes from articles 16 and 22-27 of the Universal Declaration.

43. Kirkpatrick 1990: 162, 164.

44. Article 24 of the Universal Declaration of Human Rights.

45. Cranston 1967: 51.

46. *Ibid.*, 43.

47. Kristol 1986-87: 5.

48. Which, in the view of the critics, does not preclude legitimate struggle for any social and economic rights in societies where historical conditions for acceptance and implementation of those rights are present. But this would be, in their view, a struggle not for human, but for American or French or Hungarian rights.

49. For an early, brief, seminal debate of these two views see the discussion between Charles Frankel and Walter Gellhorn in Frankel 1977: 17-27.

50. *Filartega v. Pena-Irala*, 630 F.(2nd) 876.

51. These expressions come from Sieghart 1985: 73.

52. According to article 25, "Every citizen shall have the right and the opportunity...(a) To take part in the conduct of public affairs, directly or through freely chosen representatives; (b) To vote and to be elected at genuine periodic elections which shall be by universal and equal suffrage and shall be by secret ballot, guaranteeing the free expression of the will of the electors; (c) To have access, on general terms of equality, to public service in his country." See also

Art. 3 of the Protocol No 1 to the European Convention for the Protection of Human Rights and Fundamental Freedoms (1954), and Art. 23 of the American Convention on Human Rights (1969).

53. How to understand the presumed "readiness" is a difficult question, however. For instance, should a nation's "readiness for representative government" mean that the democratic system, once established, would last without major crises or break-downs, or should it rather denote also transitions to democracy where, in the event of a crisis or breakdown, there is a reasonable degree of probability of reequilibration or restoration of democracy? For a penetrating analysis of reequilibration and restoration see Linz 1978: 14–124, esp. on pp. 87-97.

54. By being reasonable, the pursuit must be attentive to the transcending utilitarian concerns. This is particularly true of various aboriginal groups where establish-ment, often by outsiders, of a more modern government, and resort to a relentless schedule of cultural and economic change, may devastate the group, especially "through the destruction of the material basis of the community's way of life" (Donnelly 1990: 52-53).

55. The right proposed here differs from the collective right pronounced, in 1986, by the United Nations Declaration on the Right to Development. According to the relevant part of article 1/1 of that Declaration, "[t]he right to development "is an inalienable human right by virtue of which...all peoples are entitled to participate in, contribute to and enjoy economic, social, cultural and political development." (Another part of this provision, irrelevant for this discussion, declares the human right of every human person to development.) According to its critics, the very notion of "collective human rights" is self-contradictory, blurs the human rights idea, and brings about dangerous practical consequences, cf. ch. 5, n. 19, *supra*.

Clearly, the right to development which I propose here differs from its coun-terpart pronounced by the U.N. Declaration. The right proposed here would not be classified "human", and it would be explicitly established as a right of the people against the state. And it would be narrower than the U.N. peoples' right to development—it would be established to promote development to help exactly human rights incorporation. Thus, the right proposed here would be neither self-contradictory nor dangerous for individual rights.

56. The demands come, in particular, from politicians, policymakers, and interna-tional lawyers from various Third World countries. They widely accept two evalu-ative judgments. First, development, as well as self-determination, are for them the values of utmost importance. And, second, in view of their poverty, and of many past wrongs inflicted on their societies by developed nations, especially by colonial powers, the outside world has the duty to respect their self-determina-tion, political and economic, and, by sharing its wealth with them, to promote development of the former colonies. Those politicians, policymakers and lawyers do not experience these duties in a weak manner, as if they were humanitarian obligations of alms giving; they experience them as duties to which their peoples' rights correspond, and they perceive those peoples' rights as human rights (see, in particular, M'Baye 1972: 505-34, and, especialy, his "Emergence of the 'Right to Development' as a Human Right in the Context of a New International Order," [read in June 1978, at the UNESCO Conference of experts on human rights, human needs, and the establishment of a new international economic order, UNESCO Doc. SS-78/Conf. 630/8]). Thus they experience the claim for devel-opment as a moral human right, and they have been struggling until today to

make of it a legal human right as well. For instance, according to Paragraph 10 of the Declaration of the 1993 U.N. World Conference on Human Rights in Vienna, the "Conference…reaffirms the right to development as…an integral part of fundamental human rights." Moeover, a number of pargraphs reaffirm the human right to development and other human rights of the peoples in final declarations of the regional meetings for the Vienna Conference—in the Tunis Declaration of 1992 for Africa, the San Jose Declaration of 1993 for Latin America, and the Bangkok Declaration of 1993 for Asia.

Needless to say, the policy of development is of utmost importance, and so are the demands of poor societies for international assistance. They are demands against humanity, uttered in the name of the peoples suffering from poverty, hunger, deprivation. Nonetheless, it would be difficult to treat these claims as a human rights, and not only for the reasons mentioned earlier (see ch. 5, n. 19, *supra*), but also because the existing machinery of international law of human rights is unfit for the implementation of the peoples' right to development; the norms of international law of human rights, the sources of those norms, as well as public and private organizations which conduct the difficult international struggle for the rights of the human individual, would be unable to produce a sweeping world-wide change of economic policies (which includes a degree of global redistribution of wealth). Those policies require sober and persistent action of business leaders, financial institutions, and governments of industrial democracies, in cooperation with countries in need. For few business leaders, bankers, and governmental officials would the altruism of the human rights idea and the moral appeal of human rights claims provide a strong enough motivation for implementation of the difficult and costly policies; irrespective of altruism, a strong dose of rational self-interest (sometimes named "soft-core altruism" or "cost-reward altruism," cf. ch. 2, n. 99, *supra*) on the part of the helping groups and nations is necessary. No wonder that, in the words from Oscar Schachter's remarkable scrutiny of international law, "[t]he key issues of debt, trade preferences, capital flows, transfer of technology, development projects are continuously debated without any significant reference to human rights in that connection. Probably few would argue against the "right to development," but there is no indication that any specific obligations of assistance have been accepted as corollaries of that rights by those concerned with development policy in the developed countries. [Thus] it seems somewhat Utopian to suggest that human rights…can exert a force on trade, finance, and development policies" (Schachter 1991: 355). What is needed is acknowledgment, by businesses, banks and governments, of enlightened self-interest, that is, "of common interest…in combatting poverty and misery in the disdvantaged countries." This would be, in particular, the clear acknowledgment "that we are all in the same boat and must act to overcome the tragic imbalance that now exists"(*idem*).

57. Schachter 1991: 354.
58. Morgenthau 1978: 261–62.
59. The preamble and, in particular, articles 1(3), 13(1b), 55(c).
60. This controversy has been reflected in numerous court decisions. For its particularly influential articulation see the *North Sea Continental Shelf Cases* [1969] I.C.J., 4.
61. Traditionally, states have been parties to international treaties; but, in this century, an increasing number of intergovernmental organizations enjoy the status of legal persons and thus they are also able to conclude treaties with states and other

organizations. Following the few early predecessors, such as the Holy Alliance and the Pan American Union, there are hundreds of intergovernmental organizations today. Most of them are themselves established and given legal personality by international covenants, regional, as well as universal, e.g., by the pact of the League of Nations or the U. N. Charter.

62. That principle has been accepted by states for centuries, in the common belief that it is legally binding; thus, it became itself a principle of the customary international law.
63. Brownlie 1990: 12.
64. Baxter 1970: 101.
65. According to a recent estimate, the number of those in force exceeds 2,000 (Henkin, Pugh, Schachter and Smit 1993: 95-96).
66. Meron 1986: 131, 150. See also the early, groundbreaking work by W. Jenks, especially Jenks 1953.
67. Petrażycki 1959-60, vol. I, p. 241.
68. The degree of the binding force of judicial interpretation varies among legal systems, especially between the common law and civil law systems. Also interpretation by distinguished legal scholars has, in particular in the civil law tradition, a measure of authority. The most strongly binding interpretation—the "authentic" one—comes from the lawmakers themselves; this is however a rarely used kind.
69. See on this 111-12, *infra*.
70. The attempts were originally private, most conspicuously by Jeremy Bentham (cf. Keeton and Schwarzenberger 1970: 152).
71. See Brownlie 1990: 15-16.
72. In view of these controversies, the International Court of Justice (and, before 1945, the Permanent Court of International Justice) has been trying to sparingly derive some of those principles, primarily from domestic private laws and laws of procedure; its decisions refer to such principles as *res judicata, nemo iudex in re sua*, estoppel, prohibition of abuse of rights, various articulations of the clean hands requisite, the liability for nonperformance of contracts, duty to act in good faith, etc.
73. Acording to article 59, "The decision of the court has no binding force except between the parties and in respect of that particular case."
74. Falk 1964: 250.
75. Henkin 1979: 25. To be sure, Henkin himself does not despair, and he rightly asserts that "most international lawyers...(u)nable to deny the limitations of international law,...insist that these are not critical and they deny many of the alleged implications of these limitations.... They [also] reject definitions...that deny the title of law to any but the command of a sovereign, enforceable and enforced"(*ibid.*). Of course, on the last issue they are particularly correct. We have good reasons to define "law" in a largely stipulative, instrumental manner. And there are clear instrumental reasons for understanding "law" broadly enough to treat international law as "law"; this treatment, owing to the law's prestige, can only add a degree of the badly needed persuasiveness to the norms of international law. Henkin seems to implicitly accept this argument, especially on p. 329.
76. Articles 41 and 42 of the U.N. Charter.
77. Other international courts include such regional bodies as the Court of Justice of the European Community, the European Court of Human Rights, and the Inter-American Court of Human Rights.
78. Article 36 of the Statute of the Court.

79. Article 36(2) of the Statute of the Court.
80. For instance, the U.S. declaration of acceptance, in 1946, of the Court's "compulsory" jurisdiction has been qualified by the Connally Amendment (removing from the jurisdiction "disputes with regard to matters which are essentially within the domestic jurisdiction" of the U.S. as determined by the U.S.), and by a clause providing for unilateral right to terminate the declaration with six months notice—the right eventually exercised in the Nicaragua case of 1984 (1984 I.C.J. 392). On similar reservations of other countries see Henkin, Pugh, Schachter and Smit 1993: 811–812.
81. Brownlie 1990: 733.
82. Morgenthau 1978: 298.
83. For instance, in Russia, the original belief in social good as a sufficiently strong universal motivation disproved itself; at best for the theory, it disproved itself just in Russia, since Russia's level of economic and cultural development was insufficient. The disproval brought about the introduction of command economy with fear as the dominant incentive for labor. But this new, *ad hoc* theory of motivation disproved itself as well; at the best for the new theory, Russia was, in 1917, on too high a level of development for effective replacement of economic incentives by fear.
84. I owe this expression to Andrei Amalrik.
85. All voluntary organizations and independent groups were destroyed by the paralyzing fear aroused, in particular, by the terror and mass kilings of Stalinist era; with the overwhelming degree of infiltration of society by secret police and its informers, any independent contacts and communications became a threat. To be sure, in some parts of Eastern and Central Europe, Stalinism did not last long enough to entirely succeed in atomizing the society—there did survive some independent religious groups, however embattled, most conspicuously the Catholic Church. In the Soviet Union, even the family was, for a period of time, intentionally undermined as a politically dangerous group (cf. Gorecki 1972).
86. See 94, *supra*
87. Which, in this context, sounds unfortunate. But, fortunately, whatever the parents' learned characteristics, no human child will ever be born with a programmed dedication to the destruction of human rights either.
88. Heraclitus, Fragment 44.

6

Conclusion: The Importance of Justification

As indicated earlier, the importance of justification is both pragmatic and fundamental. The first of these is clear. Owing to its persuasive power, objective justification of ethics, and especially of human rights norms, is needed as a forceful source of motivation. It is needed, first, for the acquisition of moral experiences. And, once they have been acquired, it tends to reinforce their continuing strength.

The belief in the motivational power of the justification has been accepted in the first chapter. Its acceptance matches the common sense view of moral persuasion; in particular, it seems patently true that, with relatively few exceptions,[1] a speaker's moral utterance "you shouldn't kill" or "you shouldn't spare infidels" is less persuasive when understood with the addition "because I feel so," than when the utterance implies "because to do so is wrong in the most objective manner, irrespective of my or any other individual's personal opinion." To be sure, this common sense view of the power of justification has never been formally examined, and it is easy to figure out why. First, this view (and, especially, its acquisitional part) might have been too obviously true for psychologists of motivation to deserve the effort of its testing. And, most importantly, with respect to the ethos and the subsequent behavior of large groups and whole societies, no way of scrupulous testing of this view seems feasible. Their ethos and behavior are always influenced by long lists of determinants operating at various levels of causal distance, such as the group's economic circumstance, institutional conditions, internal and external conflicts, kind and level of education, intellectual tradition, and many more. All this constitutes, in Max Weber's words, spelled out in an inquiry which is only tenuously relevant for the issue at hand, a "complex interaction of innumerable different historical factors."[2] It is therefore impossible to experimentally test the issue—

there is no way of controlling all other factors to precisely determine the impact of the justification.

Nonetheless, in various areas, simple, nonexperimental observation clearly confirms the impact. This is particularly true of religious justifications underlying various fundamentalist mass movements. The movements range from the Albigensian Crusade to today's struggles for establishment of Islamic states by Moslem fundamentalists, and, on a narrower scale, to the attacks launched by Christian fundamentalists, in this country and abroad, against sexual permissiveness and, especially, abortion. When reading about and observing, on television or elsewhere, crowds of fundamentalists praying in preparation for battle against infidels, or praying, often in tears, during blockades of abortion clinics, we do experience their faith in the divine will as being a major determinant—plausibly a necessary condition—of the forcefulness of their driving experiences and subsequent struggles.

Accordingly, without a formal, experimental corroboration, the instrumental importance of objective justification of ethics has been accepted in this book. Its instrumentality may work in different ways, depending upon the contents of the ethical norms believed justified. It can help in producing fanaticism, intolerance, cruelty. But it can also operate in the opposite direction, and so it does by enhancing the human rights norms. And, from the beginning, the intrinsic, nonteleological worth of justification has been accepted in this book as well; it consists in the fundamental value of the answers dealing with ultimate questions of the human condition. When looking for the most illuminating claim of the pragmatic and fundamental value of justification, we find, in recent history, an instance of unmatched emotional and intellectual force This is the case of Gustav Radbruch, one of the greatest jurists of our time.

The Dilemma of Gustav Radbruch: Law, Positivism, and Genocide

In 1932, ten years before Janusz Korczak's deportation to Treblinka, Gustav Radbruch published in Germany the fullest acount of his legal philosophy.[3] The philosophy was well embedded in the tradition of the Enlightenment, and, in some respects, was particularly indebted to the thought of Kant.

First, Radbruch accepted Kant's resolution of the is/ought dilemma: "Kantian philosophy has taught us that it is impossible from what is to logically derive...what ought to be."[4] Accordingly, statements concerning the ought "may only be based deductively on statements of the same kind," whereas the ultimate statements concerning the ought, which the individual "draws from...his conscience...are incapable of proof, axiomatic"; thus, by being untestable, they are out of the field of science.[5] Radbruch named this view of evaluative judgments "relativism," and the view seems to sound like acceptance of the positivistic demarcation line between propositions of scientific knowledge and of what many positivists perceive as metaphysical babble.

But Radbruch was not a philosophical positivist and, especially, not a logical positivist of his day. His agnosticism went far enough to admit, in accord with the positivists, that the ultimate, untestable questions of human condition, existential and evaluative, cannot be answered in a publicly convincing manner. But neither Radbruch nor other Neo-Kantian philosophers accept the positivist and, especially, the neopositivist convention on meaning which renders all the attempted answers to these questions a meaningless nonsense. Radbruch's writings display consistently his conviction that these questions and answers are of utmost importance; he accepts "a renunciation of the scientific establishment of ultimate decisions [but] not a renunciation of the decision itself."[6] In particular, his claim "that judgments of value cannot be scientifically proved...is radically different from the proposition that they do not matter."[7]

Accordingly, Radbruch (building on the work of Dilthey and such Kantians as Rickert, Windelband and Lask) accepted a nonpositivistic definition and classification of scientific knowledge. To be sure, the natural sciences should be perceived, in his view, as a body of value free, testable propositions. In contrast, the philosophy of values, including legal philosophy, is explicitly evaluative. And in between there are humanities and *Sozialwissenschaften*—the "cultural sciences" in Radbruch's terminology, that is, the disciplines dealing with creations of the human mind understood by him as "culture"; they are so closely related to values that their reduction to the testable is impossible. Legal science is among them, since "law is a creation of man, and like any human creation it can be understood only by its idea," that is, the idea which the creation is to serve.[8]

What is the "idea of law"? When analyzing it in the book under discussion Radbruch came close, despite his explicitly antipositivist philosophical stand, to a virtual acceptance of legal positivism. He finds the idea of law in three categories of values: justice, teleology (aimed at a few ultimate values), and certainty. He deals with justice first, since justice is the specific (even though not the only) value that law is to serve—in accord with its *a priori* concept, "law is the reality the meaning of which is to serve justice."[9] Basically, he understands justice in a manner following the Aristotelian notion: treat equal cases alike and different cases according to relevant differences among them.[10] However, thus defined, "justice" has a narrow denotation.[11] And, as Radbruch admits, it is a formal term, the precise meaning of which varies from one culture (and sometimes one group or even person) to another; the definition does not determine which differences are relevant,[12] and "it determines solely the relation, and not the kind of the treatment."[13] The meaning of justice can be specified only by addition of the second, culturally variable component of the idea of law, that is, the teleology aimed at implementation of the society's ultimate value or values.[14] In Radbruch's view, human societies cherish three ultimate social goods— the individual human personality, the human collectivity, and the creations of civilization (such as works of arts or sciences). Some societies aim more forcefully at the implementation of individualism, others—of various kinds of collectivism, and still others—at the development of civilization; and in each of them the specific meaning of justice may be different. Needless to say, in many, if not all, societies the three kinds of valuations coexist and easily clash with each other, and thus the specific meaning of justice becomes controversial. These (and other) controversies generate the third essential component of the idea of law, that is, legal certainty; the "law as the order of living together cannot be handed over to disagreements between the views of individuals; it must be one order over all of them."[15] Legal certainty is essential for avoidance of conflicts of rights, that is, for social peace. Moreover, to a degree, the certainty is itself a prerequisite for justice—"like treatment of like cases" demands uniform and consistent distribution of rewards and punishments, rights and burdens;[16] thus, there is a limited extent of convergence between certainty and justice.

Despite the convergence, the three components of the idea of law unavoidably contradict each other. In particular, justice demands treating like cases alike, whereas teleological considerations often beg, in the name of policies, for differential treatment.[17] And legal certainty—the demand that law be uniformly applied—clashes with justice or teleology whenever the law, owing to its general articulation, runs, in an individual case or peculiar kind of cases, against prerequisites of justice or against a policy in need.

Which of these conflicting principles should ultimately prevail? Radbruch admits that "different ages will be inclined to lay decisive stress upon one or the other of those principles."[18] He himself claimed, in 1932, legal certainty to be the controlling value. The very existence of a legal order depends upon legal certainty which only positive law can provide, and thus bring peace "betwen conflicting legal views" and terminate "the struggle of all against all." And the "existence of the legal order is more important than its justice and expediency.... It is "more important *that* the strife of legal views be ended than that it be determined *justly* and *expediently*."[19] To be sure, "there may be 'shameful laws' which consciense refuses to obey. [But it] is the professional duty of the judge...to sacrifice his own sense of the right to the authoritative command of the law, to ask only what is legal and not if it is also just... We despise the parson who preaches in a sense contrary to his conviction, but we respect the judge who does not permit himself to be diverted from his loyalty to the law by his conflicting sense of the right."[20]

In this manner Radbruch, even though otherwise critical of legal positivism, resolved the problem of the contradictions in a purely positivist way.[21] The state-made norms of positive law are law, right or wrong, purposeful or purposeless; in other words, the lawyer's law is law. All other concerns, especially moral and teleological, are the business of policymakers and lawmakers, whereas the role of legal craftsmen—judges, prosecutors, defense lawyers—is only to conduct the systemic analysis and scrupulous application of the state-made provisions in force. This prescription refers even to the "shameful laws which conscience refuses to obey." But the example of a German "shameful law" he was able to provide was relatively mild.[22] Despite the ominous signs, Radbruch perceived Europe as if it still were a cradle of liberalism and legality, and a continuation of the great tradition of over a century of scientific, technological, and social progress, justifying the optimistic faith in basic human decency and power of reason. Clearly, he was unable to anticipate the character of the positive law soon to come—of the new shameful laws to be implemented in Germany and in most of Europe.

In 1933 his world crumbled, and Radbruch went into internal exile. On May 9, 1933, on the ground of a Nazi statute enacted a month earlier, he was dismissed from his professorship at Heidelberg; according to the letter of dismissal, "his whole personality and his political activities to date do not guarantee that he will now support the national state without reservations."[23] Over the course of the following twelve years, Radbruch witnessed the unheard of horrors committed in the name of positive law—a positive law where "murder of political opponents amounts to virtue, murder of members of another race is commended, whereas a similar act aimed at own political companions is sanctioned by the most dreadful and degrading penalties."[24] And, what he found particularly shocking was the degree to which legal positivism and its rejection of absolute ethics contributed to the implementation of the totalitarian rule. In his words published after the fall of Germany, the German lawyer "knows, nearly two hundred years since the death of the last adherents of natural law among the jurists, that there are no... exceptions from the validity and binding force of positive law...the right thing to do is to obey the law, whatever it orders."[25] Thus, "legal positivism...unable, on its own, to provide the [deeper, ethical] justification of legal norms...maintains to prove validity of an enacted law by the power backing the law's effective enforcement, [even though] power can possibly provide ground for a must, but never for an ought."[26] Which, according to Radbruch's experience, brought about, in 1933 and after, a genuine disaster: "This understanding of law and of its validity has made the lawyers and the nation defenseless against enacted laws, however arbitrary, however cruel, however criminal those laws were."[27]

This was the main reason why Radbruch proclaimed, for post-Nazi Germany, "a struggle against positivism"[28]—a struggle to be conducted from the standpoint of the "statutory lawlessness and the law higher than statutes."[29] And even though he still professed the importance of certainty and positivity,[30] it became clear for him that certainty, however important, was not to be held as the determinative value of the idea of law; the controlling role should rather go to justice. Accordingly, he proposed a new way of resolving the conflict between legal certainty and justice. In his view,

[p]reference should be given to the rule of positive law...even when the rule is unjust...unless the violation of justice reaches so intolerable a degree that the rule becomes in effect "lawless law" and must therefore yield to justice. It is impossible to draw a sharper line between the cases where enactment must give way to justice and those where a law must be recognized as valid despite its hurtful and unjust contents. There is, however, one line of distinction that can be drawn with

complete clarity. Where there is not even an attempt at justice, where equality, which is the core of justice, is deliberately repudiated in the establishment of a rule of positive law, then the rule is not merely wrong but lacks the very nature of law. For law...cannot be otherwise defined than as an institution or ordering of human relations the meaning and purpose of which is to serve justice. Measured by this standard whole portions of the National Socialist legislation never attained the rank of valid law.[31]

These words provide no clear criterion of validity, but only "one line of distinction" dealing with a lack of "even an attempt at justice." But, in a number of further comments, Radbruch articulates the prerequisites for validity of positive law in a new and wider manner; now they include also, besides qualified equality, other components of "justice" understood in a broader, more ordinary sense,[32] such as legality, especially on the part of the administration of justice, absence of full concentration of power in the hands of a totalitarian "party,"[33] respect for human rights, in particular for the right to life, liberty, and honor,[34] as well as rights of the defendant to fairness of criminal law and procedure.[35]

In this manner Radbruch, departing from legal positivism (and even from his version of relativism), proclaims, under the name of "higher law," a minimum set of absolute, universally binding moral norms as prerequisite for the validity of positive law. This proclamation accepts objective moral justification of the norms of law. And, most importantly for these considerations, it amounts to clear recognition of absolute, objectively justified morality underlying law, that is, to the acceptance of objective justification of morality itself.

How and where did Radbruch find the objective justification of ethics? His search was strenuous and largely inconclusive. Some of his students claim that, having died in 1949, he did not live long enough to conclude it. Others blame not just his death, but also the perennial difficulty "of the search of mankind for absolute justice"—the difficulty encountered by "all fundamental philosophies;" and they stress that in Radbruch's case, the difficulty was magnified by "the tension between faith and scepticism that accompanies the life and work of this noble man and philosopher."[36] In the course of his search, Radbruch was referring, with utmost difficulty and hesitation, to various major normmaking facts accepted, in the past, by others,[37] and he ultimately claimed that to endow "the lawyers and the nation" with a forceful defense against tyrannical outrage, "[l]egal philosophy must restore to consciousness a wisdom that is centuries old and that was common to antiquity, the Christian Middle Ages and the Enlightenment. During these periods men believed that there was a law higher than mere enactment, which they called the law of Nature, the law of God, or the law of Reason. Measured by this higher law, lawlessness remains lawlessness when accomplished through legal forms; wrong remains wrong though enacted in a statute."[38]

The Importance of Justification

Radbruch's departure from legal positivism and his strenuous search for absolute justice provides a dramatic instance of the problem under scrutiny—the importance of objective justification of ethics (and, subsequently, law). Again, the reasons for this importance are pragmatic and fundamental, with the former consisting in the justification's motivating power. We saw how Radbruch perceived the positivist rejection of absolute ethics as a major determinant of the easiness with which, in 1933, the totalitarian rule won; the rejection "has made the lawyers and the nation defenseless" against the cruelties of the new provisions. That is why, for a stronger defense against tyranny, lawyers and nations do need the forceful motivation provided by objectively justified ethical norms—the norms higher than mere enactment.

This instrumental value of objective justification can be claimed by advocates of any moral norm or moral system. But moral norms spread and take hold over societies with variable degrees of difficulty. Clearly, the higher the degree of the difficulty for a given set of norms, the greater the need of the justification. This is particularly true of human rights norms; we have seen how many odds must be overcome for their worldwide implementation. Among the odds there is the power of various group interests running against the human rights idea, especially ethnic, economic, religious, and political interests; underdevelopment in many areas; forceful defense of traditional sovereignty, especially on the part of the despotically governed states; the vagueness of the sources and weakness of enforcement of the international law of human rights, making it a largely impotent normative system; and, most notably, the fact that even if, having overcome all these dilemmas, the world reached a universal implementation of human rights, the triumph would not be irreversible, and thus the struggle would have to continue with no end in sight, from generation to generation. Thus, bearing these difficulties in mind, the increase of persuasiveness of the human rights idea and the resulting rise of its motivating power seem invaluable.

But there is more than just teleology here. The objective justification had been perceived by Radbruch and many others as invaluable for fundamental reasons as well. For thousands of years humans have been asking, often in bewilderment, the most basic questions dealing with the ultimate nature and meaning of the world, of life, and of the human condition. Many of these questions seek answers articulated as statements of fact. But there are among them also the evaluative questions—on what ought to be done or avoided as ultimately right or wrong, and where does the ultimate oughtness come from. The answers to these ethical and metaethical questions deal with an essential part of the nature of the world and of our condition. Thrown into the world, we persistently ask these questions, and we do cherish the ceaseless search for the answers, and, above all, the answers themselves. These answers have for us the fundamental, nonteleological value, and so does, in particular, the answer to the problem of justification.

Notes

1. That is, unless, owing to authoritarian character of the culture, of a peculiar personal relationship, or both, the utterer of a moral view has unusual moral authority over the addressee.
2. *The Protestant Ethic and the Spirit of Capitalism* (Weber 1958: 90). The inquiry—a part of Weber's broader analysis of the social impact of ideas and religious beliefs—may look, *prima facie*, as if it contained an effort to examine the instrumental power of the objective justification. Weber scrutinized some Protestant sects, especially the orthodox Calvinists of the sixteenth and seventeenth centuries, to show how the requirements of their faith have made the duties of "inner-wordly asceticism"—hard work, frugal lifestyle, and capital accumulation—a virtue, and thus became a critical determinant of the birth of modern capitalism and, consequently, of the economic and cultural development of the West. This scrutiny might be perceived as an effort to demonstrate how divine orders can stimulate, in business, a new moral motivation strong enough to bring about a sweeping social change—that is, an effort to demonstrate the persuasive power of religious justification of moral norms.

 This perception would be incorrect, however. Whether the Weberian religious explanation of modern capitalism is well founded is a controversial issue debated with unusual intensity for over eighty years. But even if true, the explanation demonstrates the persuasive power of religious teleology rather than of the religious justification of ethics. In Weber's view, the doctrine of predestination (in conjunction with the transcendence of the Calvinist God) made a believer's afterlife an unknown issue, determined in advance by unconstrained and humanly incomprehensible divine will. Thus, the Calvinists were unable to earn salvation by personal worth, faith, prayer, or however they behaved, and, consequently, none of them knew whether his or her place would be among the blessed or the doomed. The outcome was, in Weber's view, an overwhelming fear, with everyone asking anxiously: what will my ultimate destination be? The Calvinist divines found a way of alleviating the anxiety; they specified the signs of God's grace which indicated the future. These signs were: an ascetic lifestyle leading, through relentless work and thrift, to accumulation of capital; the greater the success in accumulating wealth in this manner, the clearer the sign. Thus, the Puritan motivation of that early period was, according to Weber (even though not to some of his critics, most notably R.H. Tawney), teleological rather than moral—driven by fear, they behaved as exhorted, in order to find out that they were among the blessed, that is, to come as close as possible to the certainty of personal salvation. That is why the relevance of *Protestant Ethic* for the issue under discussion is tenuous. The book, as well as its long-lasting criticism, are significant here in one important way, however. They show that it is hardly feasible to establish, in publicly convincing manner, one specific critical determinant of a sweeping societal change.

3. *Rechtsphilosophie*, 3rd (completely remade) edition,1932. The following quotations from the book come from an English translation. The translation was published in 1950, and I will refer to it as "Radbruch 1950."
4. Radbruch 1950: 53.
5. *Ibid.*, 53, 55, 57.
6. *Ibid.*, 58.
7. Friedmann 1967: 196, n. 10.
8. Radbruch 1950: 51, 52, 73.
9. *Ibid.*, 75, 77.
10. *Ibid.*, 74-75, 90-91, 107-8.
11. It is much narrower than that accepted in common language. What do we mean when saying: "this schoolboy is being punished by his principal justly" or "this principal is a just person" or "norm X pronounced by the principal is just"? We refer in such statements to acts or character of, or to norms pronounced by, those in power who distribute rewards and punishments, goods and burdens. When making the first assertion we mean that a person or institution in power has performed a distribution in a way that we evaluate as morally right: we experience his duty to perform it in this way. When making the second, we mean that a person or institution in power always makes distributions that we evaluate as morally right. When making the last, we mean that a norm enacted by a powerholder orders a distribution that we evaluate as morally right. Thus, any society or social group calls a distribution of rewards or punishments "just" if the distribution matches moral experiences prevailing in the group, and it calls a person in power "just" if he coninuously performs the just distributions.

    Since moral sentiments of various societies differ, the same distribution may be just in one society and unjust in another. There is a limitation to this variability, however: one moral demand referring to the distributions seems to be constant. This is the claim that each distribution be made according to uniform criteria, that is, in Radbruch's articulation, the claim of treating like cases alike, and different cases according to relevant differences among them. Thus, Radbruch's definition, limiting justice to consistency, is narrow—it denotes only one component of what is commonly understood as "justice" (Cf. on this Gorecki 1979: 20-22).

12. In Radbruch's words, "while justice directs us to treat equals equally, unequals unequally, it does not tell us anything about the viewpoint from which they are to be deemed equals or unequals...equality is but an abstraction...taken from a certain point of view" (Radbruch 1950: 107, 109).

13. *Ibid.*, 107-8.

14. I use here the term "teleology" which is closer to Radbruch's *"Zweckmässigkeit"* than "expediency" used by Kurt Wilk in the American translation of Radbruch's book or "utility" used in a few passages translated by Lon Fuller (cf., in particular, Fuller 1954: 483 n. 48); "expediency" has too broad a connotation, whereas "utility"—too narrow, by vaguely implying utilitarian values only. However, when quoting in the upcoming text passages from Wilk's translation, I follow his terminology.

15. Radbruch 1950: 108.

16. *Ibid.*

17. This contradiction "is illustrated, for instance, by the conflict between administration and administrative courts [or] the struggle between the tendencies of justice and expediency in criminal law," *ibid.*, 109.

18. *Ibid.*, 111. He continues: so the government of enlightened despotism "sought to raise the principle of expediency to sole dominion, unhesitatingly pushing aside justice and legal certainty in its administration of law by cabinet fiats. So the age of natural law tried to conjure the entire contents of the law out of the formal principle of justice and at the same time therefrom to derive the validity of law."

19. *Ibid*, 108, 118.

20. *Ibid.*, 118-19.

21. In his words (apparently indebted to Petrażycki's work published earlier in Germany, especially Petrażycki 1895), "with fatal one-sidedness, the past age of legal positivism saw only the positivity and certainty of the law and caused a long standstill in the systematic examination of the expediency, not to mention the justice, of enacted law, for decades nearly silencing legal philosophy and legal policy" (Radbruch 1950: 111). However, there is here no inconsistency on Radbruch's part—he challenges the positivist rejection of legal philosophy and of legal policy for the use of lawmakers, but recommends the positivist legal practice.

22. It was the response to anti-socialist statute of 1878-1890 by a convention of the German Social Democrats; the convention resolved that "the party strives for its aims by *all* means, and no longer merely by all *legal* means" (Radbruch 1950: 118-19).

23. Wolf 1963: 57-58.

24. Radbruch [1945] 1963: 335, 336.

25. *Ibid.*, 335.

26. Radbruch [1946] 1963: 352.

27. Radbruch [1945] 1963: 355; similarly, Radbruch 1965: 113. See also Schneider 1968: 405-42, esp. 424-33.

28. Radbruch [1946] 1963: 352.

29. *Ibid.*, 352; the last few words quoted are a translation of the title of Radbruch's article (Radbruch [1946] 1963). ("Gesetzliches Unrecht und übergesetzliches Recht," was originally published in 1946 in 1 *Süddeutsche Zeitung*, 105, and subsequently reprinted in Radbruch 1963.)

30. "[A]ny positive law brings by itself, irrespective of its contents, some value; it is always better than no law at all, since it provides, at least, legal certainty...And it must not be overlooked—exactly in view of the experience of the twelve [Nazi] years—what terrible dangers...can the notion of "statutory lawlessness"—the denial of legality of positive law—bring" (*Ibid.*, 352, 354).
31. *Ibid.*, 353 (translated by Fuller 1954: 384–85).
32. Cf. ch. 6, n. 11, *supra*.
33. Radbruch [1946] 1963: 348, 354.
34. *Ibid.*, 351, 354; Radbruch 1965: 98; [1945] 1963: 336; 1947: 9.
35. Radbruch [1946] 1963: 354; 1965: 99.
36. Friedmann 1967: 95 and 194, n. 6. The expression "between faith and scepticism" comes from Radbruch's, *Theodor Fontane—Skepsis und Glaube*, set secretly in type in Leipzig, by Koehler & Amelang, in 1943–44, to appear only in 1946 (Cf. Wolf 1963: 65–67).
37. When debating those normmaking facts, he sometimes seemed close to their skeptical rejection, and, on other occasions, close to their acceptance. This was particularly true of his reference to nature as the source of natural law; even though as late as in 1934 he was still challenging the idea of natural law from both empirical and epistemological perspective (in Radbruch 1957: 80–81; this was a German edition of an article originally published in France, in 1934), he came, in the wake of the subsequent experience of the Nazi rule, close to genuine acceptance of natural law as the "higher law" determining the validity of positive law: "following the century of legal positivism, the idea of the law higher than statutes is powerful again, that is, of the law under which the enacted statutes may appear to be statutory lawlessness .... Natural law...[provides]...the answer to the question of what are the criteria for validity of enacted statutes" (Radbruch 1965: 114; cf. also Radbruch [1945] 1963: 335, 336, and Radbruch 1947). Furthermore, Radbruch struggled strenuously with the dilemma of religious justification. Born in a Lutheran family, Radbruch grew up, in his words, "without any relationship to religion" (Wolf 1958: 21). But he was reverent, and his yearning for religion, reemerging in his life and work, became a major concern of his later years. And eventually, in accord with his non-dogmatic deist predilection, he professed the "*anima naturaliter christiana* [in] the last sentence of his farewell address to his students" (Wolf 1963: 77). However, despite the reverence with which he treated faith and, in particular, religious moral and legal philosophy, he was, in his publications, respectfully describing rather than accepting the religious stand; accordingly, he never went as far as to endorse the divine will as the binding source of moral and legal norms. "Endowed with a soberly critical mind" (Wolf 1958: 10) and afraid of religious fanaticism, he was too much of a survivor of the Enlightenment and of a believer in the idea of ethical autonomy to opt for this kind of endorsement.
38. Radbruch 1947, translated by Fuller 1954: 484.

Bibliography

Alexander, Richard D. 1979. *Darwinism and Human Affairs*. Seattle: University of Washington Press.

_____. 1987. *The Biology of Moral Systems*. New York: Aldine de Gruyter.

Almond, Gabriel A. and Sidney Verba. 1963. *The Civic Culture*, Princeton: Princeton University Press.

Aquinas, St. Thomas. 1954. *Summa Theologica*. New York: Random House.

Asch, Solomon E. 1951. "Effects of Group Pressure upon the Modification and Distortion of Judgment." In H. Guetzkow, ed., *Groups, Leadership and Men*. Pittsburgh: The Carnegie Press.

_____. 1952. *Social Psychology*. New York: Prentice Hall.

_____. 1968. "Gestalt Theory," In 6, *International Encyclopedia of Social Science*.

Ayer, A.J. 1950. *Language, Truth and Logic*, London: Gollancz.

_____. 1984. *Freedom and Morality and Other Essays*. Oxford: Clarendon Press.

Barash, David P. 1982. *Sociobiology and Behavior*. New York: Elsevier.

Baxter, Richard R. 1970. "Treaties and Custom." 129 *Rec. des Cours*.

Bay, Christian. 1982. "Self-Respect as a Human Right: Thoughts on the Dialectics of Wants and Needs in the Struggle for Human Community." 4:1 *Human Rights Quarterly*.

Bentham, Jeremy. 1970. *Jeremy Bentham and the Law*, W. Keeton and George Schwarzenberger, eds. Westport, CT: Greenwood Press.

Benedict, Ruth. 1934. *Patterns of Culture*. Boston: Houghton Mufflin.

Brandt, Richard B. 1959. *Ethical Theory*. Englewood Cliffs, NJ: Prentice Hall.

_____. 1979. *A Theory of the Good and the Right*. Oxford: Clarendon Press.

Brownlie, Ian. 1988. "The Rights of Peoples in Modern International Law." In *The Rights of Peoples*, James Crawford, ed. Oxford: Clarendon Press.

_____. 1990. *Principles of Public International Law*. Oxford: Clarendon Press.

Cicero. 1928. *De Legibus*. Loeb Classical Library, London: Heinemann.

Corner, George W., ed. 1948. *The Autobiography of Benjamin Franklin*, Memoirs of the American Philosophical Society, vol.25. Princeton: Princeton University Press.

139

Cranston, Maurice. 1967. "Human Rights, Real and Supposed." In *Political Theory and the Rights of Man*. Bloomington: Indiana University Press.

Crick, Francis. 1966. *Of Molecules and Men*. Seattle: University of Washington Press.

Dahl, Robert A. 1971. *Polyarchy: Participation and Opposition*. New Haven: Yale University Press.

Darley, John M. and Thomas R. Shultz. 1990. "Moral Rules: Their Content and Aquisition." In 41 *Annual Review of Psychology*.

Darwin, Charles. 1896. *The Descent of Man*. New York: D. Appleton.

Diamond, Larry, Juan J. Linz, and Seymour M. Lipset. eds. 1988-9. *Democracy in Developing Countries* (volumes 2, 3, and 4 dealing, respectively, with Africa, Asia, and Latin America). Boulder, CO: Lynne Rienner.

Dickemann, Mildred. 1979. "Female Infanticide, Reproductive Strategies, and Social Stratification: A Preliminary Model." In Napoleon A. Chagnon and William Irons, eds., *Evolutionary Biology and Human Social Behavior*. Belmont: Wadsworth.

Dobzhansky, Theodosius. 1974. "Natural Selection and Pseudoselection." In Francesco Jose Ayala and Theodosius Dobzhansky, eds., *Studies in the Philosophy of Biology*. Berkeley: University of California Press.

Donat, Alexander. 1979. *The Death Camp Treblinka—A Documentary*. New York: Holocaust Library.

Donnelly, Jack. 1989. *Universal Human Rights in Theory and Practice*. Ithaca, NY: Cornell University Press.

_____. 1990. "Human Rights, Individual Rights and Collective Rights." In Jan Berting and Peter R. Baehr, eds., *Human Rights in a Pluralist World*. Roosevelt Study Center Publication No.10. Westport, CT: Meckler.

Dovidio John F. 1984. "Helping Behavior and Altruism: An Empirical and Conceptual Overview." In Leonard Berkowitz, ed., 17, *Advances in Experimental Social Psychology*. Orlando: Academic Press.

Duncker, Karl. 1939. "Ethical Relativity," 48 *Mind*.

Durkheim, Emile. 1938. *The Rules of Sociological Method*. Glencoe, IL: The Free Press.

_____. 1965. "The Determination of Moral Facts." In *Sociology and Philosophy*. London: Cohen and West.

Dworkin, Ronald. 1977. *Taking Rights Seriously*. Cambridge, MA: Harvard University Press.

Falk, Richard A. 1964. "The Adequacy of Contemporary Theories of International Law—Gaps in Legal Thinking." 50 *Virginia Law Review*.

Feinberg, Joel. 1970. "The Nature and Value of Rights." 4 *The Journal of Value Inquiry*.

Foot, Philippa. 1978. *Virtues and Vices*. Berkeley: University of California Press.

Frankena, William K. 1963. *Ethics*. Englewood Cliffs, NJ: Prentice Hall.

Frankel, Charles. 1977. "Human Rights and Imperialism." In *Human Rights— A Symposium, 6/1 Procedings of the General Education Seminar*. New York: Columbia University.

Frenkel-Brunswick, Else. 1954. "Social Research and the Problem of Values: A Reply." 49 *Journal of Abnormal and Social Psychology*.

Friedmann Wolfgang. 1967. *Legal Theory*. New York: Columbia University Press.

Fuller, Lon. 1954. "American Legal Philosophy at Mid-Century." 6 *Journal of Legal Education*.

Garrod, Andrew, ed. 1993. *Approaches to Moral Development: New Research and Emerging Themes*. New York: Teachers College Press.

Gellhorn, Walter. 1960. *American Rights*. New York: Macmillan.

Gellner, Ernest. 1992. *Reason and Culture*. Oxford: Blackwell.

Gewirth, Alan. 1978. *Reason and Morality*. Chicago: University of Chicago Press.

_____. 1984. *Human Rights: Essays on Justification and Applications*. Chicago: University of Chicago Press.

Ginsberg, Morris. 1965. *On Justice in Society*. Ithaca, NY: Cornell University Press.

Gorecki, Jan. 1972. "Communist Family Pattern: Law as an Implement of Change." *University of Illinois Law Forum*.

_____. 1979. *A Theory of Criminal Justice*. New York: Columbia University Press.

_____. 1983. *Capital Punishment*. New York: Columbia University Press.

Gross, Paul R. and Norman Levitt. 1994. *Higher Superstition: The Academic Left and Its Quarrels with Science*. Baltimore: Johns Hopkins University Press.

Grotius, Hugo. [1625] 1853. *De Jure Belli ac Pacis*, vol. 1. Cambridge: Cambridge University Press.

Hare, R.M. 1963. *Freedom and Reason*. Oxford: Clarendon Press.

_____. 1981. *Moral Thinking*. Oxford: Clarendon Press.

Hart, H.L.A. 1961. *The Concept of Law*. Oxford: Clarendon Press.

Hempel, Carl G. 1965. *Aspects of Scientific Explanation*. New York: The Free Press.

Henkin, Louis. 1978. *The Rights of Man Today*. Boulder, CO: Westview Press.

_____. 1979. *How Nations Behave*. New York: Columbia University Press.

_____, Richard C. Pugh, Oscar Schachter, and Hans Smit. 1993. *International Law: Cases and Materials*. St. Paul: West.

Herskovits, Melville. 1948. *Man and His Works*. New York: Alfred A. Knopf.

Hoffman, Martin L. 1970. "Moral Development." In Paul H. Mussen, ed., *Carmichael's Handbook of Child Psychology*, vol. 2. New York: Wiley.

_____. 1977. "Moral Internalization: Current Theory and Research." In Leonard Berkowitz, ed., 10, *Advances in Experimental Social Psychology.* New York: Academic Press.

_____. 1993. "Empathy, Social Cognition, and Moral Education." In Andrew Garrod, ed., *Approaches to Moral Development: New Research and Emerging Themes.* New York: Teachers College Press.

Hopkins, Keith. 1980. "Brother-Sister Marriage in Roman Egypt." 22 *Comparative Studies in Society and History.*

Horowitz, Irving Louis. 1993. *The Decomposition of Sociology.* New York: Oxford University Press.

Inkeles, Alex and Daniel J. Levinson. 1968. "National Character: The Study of Modal Personality and Sociocultural Systems." In Gardner Lindzey and Elliot Aronson, eds., *The Handbook of Social Psychology*, vol. 4. Reading, MA: Addison-Wesley.

Jacob, François. 1973. *The Logic of Life: A History of Heredity.* New York: Pantheon Books.

Jenks, W. 1953. "The Conflict of Law-Making Treaties." 30 *British Yearbook of International Law.*

John Paul II. 1994. *Crossing the Threshold of Hope.* New York: Alfred A. Knopf.

Kalinowski, Georges. 1967. *Le probleme de la verité en morale et en droit.* Lyon: Emmanuel Vitte.

Kant, Immanuel. [1785] 1959. *Foundations of the Metaphysics of Morals.* Indianapolis: Bobbs-Merrill.

Kaye, Howard L. 1986. *The Social Meaning of Modern Biology.* New Haven: Yale University Press.

Kirkpatrick, Jeane. 1990. "Establishing a Viable Human Rights Policy." In Walter Laqueur and Barry Rubin, eds., *The Human Rights Reader.* New York: Meridian.

Kluckhohn, Clyde. 1955. "Ethical Relativity: *Sic et Non.*" 52 *Journal of Philosophy.*

Kohlberg, L. 1981. *Essays on Moral Development*, vol. 1: *The Philosophy of Moral Development.* San Francisco: Harper and Row.

_____. 1984. *Essays in Moral Development*, vol. 2: *The Psychology of Moral Development.* San Francisco: Harper and Row.

Korczak, Janusz. 1978. *Ghetto Diary.* New York: Holocaust Library.

Kristol, Irving. 1986-87. "Human Rights: The Hidden Agenda." 6 *The National Interest.*

Kymlicka, Will and Wayne Norman. 1994. "Return of the Citizen: A Survey of Recent Work on Citizenship Theory." 104 *Ethics.*

Lande, Jerzy. 1959. *Studia z filozofii prawa* (Studies in Legal Philosophy). Warsaw: P.W.N.

_____. 1975. "The Sociology of Petrażycki." In Jan Gorecki, ed., *Sociology and Jurisprudence of Leon Petrażycki*. Urbana: University of Illinois Press.

Larenz, K. 1983. *Methodenlehre der Rechtswissenschaft*. Berlin: Springer.

Latane, B. and J.M. Darley. 1970. *The Unresponsive Bystander: Why Doesn't He Help*. New York: Appleton Century Crofts.

Lauterpacht, Hersch. 1950. *International Law and Human Rights*. London: Stevens and Sons.

Lazari-Pawłowska, Ija. 1970. "Moralność a natura ludzka" (Morality and Human Nature). 6 *Etyka*.

Lerner, Daniel. 1958. *The Passing of Traditional Society*. Glencoe, IL: The Free Press.

Lijphart, Arend. 1977. *Democracy in Plural Societies: A Comparative Exploration*. New Haven: Yale University Press.

_____. 1984. *Democracies: Patterns of Majoritarian and Consensus Government in Twenty-One Countries*. New Haven: Yale University Press.

Linton, Ralph. 1952. "Universal Ethical Principles: An Anthropological View." In Ruth Nanda Anshen, ed., *Moral Principles of Action*. New York: Harper.

_____. 1954. "The Problem of Universal Values." In Robert F. Spencer, ed., *Method and Perspective in Anthropology*. Minneapolis: University of Minnesota Press.

Linz, Juan J. 1978. "Crisis, Breakdown, and Reequilibration." In Juan J. Linz and Alfred Stepan, eds., *The Breakdown of Democratic Regimes*. Baltimore: Johns Hopkins University Press.

Lipset, Seymour Martin. 1959. "Some Social Requisites of Democracy." 53 *American Political Science Review*.

_____. [1959] 1981. *Political Man*. Baltimore: Johns Hopkins University Press.

_____. 1994. "The Social Requisites of Democracy Revisited." 59 *American Sociological Review*.

_____. and Stein Rokkan, eds. 1967. *Party Systems and Voter Allignments: Crossnational Perspectives*. New York: Free Press.

Locke, John. [1690] 1924. *Of Civil Government*. London: J.M. Dent and Sons.

Lumsden, Charles J. and Edward O. Wilson. 1981. *Genes, Mind and Culture*. Cambridge, MA: Harvard University Press.

_____. 1983. *Promethean Fire*. Cambridge, MA: Harvard University Press.

MacIntyre, Alasdair. [1959] 1969. "Hume on 'is' and 'ought.'" In W.D. Hudson, ed., *The Is/Ought Question*. London: Macmillan.

_____. 1984. *After Virtue*. Notre Dame, IN: Notre Dame University Press.

Mackie, J.L. 1977. *Ethics: Inventing Right and Wrong*. Harmondsworth: Penguin.

Malinowski, Bronislaw. [1944] 1960. *A Scientific Theory of Culture*. New York: Oxford University Press.

Maslow, Abraham H. 1959. "Psychological Data and Value Theory." In Abraham H. Maslow, ed., *New Knowledge in Human Values*. New York: Harper and Brothers.

_____. 1970. *Motivation and Personality*. New York: Harper and Row.

_____. 1976. *The Farther Reaches of Human Nature*. New York: The Viking Press.

M'Baye, Keba. 1972. "Le droit au developpement comme un droit de l'homme." 5 *Revue des droits de l'homme*.

Meron, Theodor. 1986. *Human Rights Law-Making in the United Nations*. Oxford: Clarendon Press.

Merton, Robert K. 1968. *Social Theory and Social Structure*. New York: The Free Press.

Milgram, S. 1970. "The Experience of Living in Cities." 167 *Science*.

Mill, John Stuart. [1863] 1972. *Utilitarianism, Liberty, Representative Government*, H.B. Acton, ed., London: J. M. Dent and Sons.

Monod, François. 1969. *From Biology to Ethics*. San Diego: Salk Institute for Biological Studies.

_____. 1971. *Chance and Necessity*. New York: Alfred A. Knopf.

Morgenthau, Hans J. 1978. *Politics Among Nations*. New York: Alfred A. Knopf.

Nahlik, Stanisław. 1967. *Wstęp do nauki prawa miedzynarodowego* (Introduction to International Law). Warszawa: P.W.N.

Nowak, Stefan. 1968. "Stanisław Ossowski." 11, *International Encyclopedia of Social Science*.

Ossowska, Maria. 1971. *Social Determinants of Moral Ideas*. London: Routledge and Kegan Paul.

Ossowski, Stanisław. 1967. "Z nastrojów manichejskich" (Manichean Predilections). In *Z zagadnien psychologii społecznej* (On Social Psychology). Warsaw: P.W.N.

Peczenik, Alexander. 1983. The Basis of Legal Justification, Lund.

Petrażycki, Leon. 1895. *Die Lehre vom Einkommen*. Berlin: H.W. Mueller.

_____. [1905, in Russian] 1959. *Wstęp do nauki prawa i moralności* (Introduction to Law and Morality). Warsaw: P.W.N.

_____. [1909-10, in Russian] 1959-60. *Teoria państwa i prawa* (Theory of State and Law). Warsaw: P.W.N.

_____. 1955. *Law and Morality*. Cambridge, MA: Harvard University Press.

_____. 1985. *O nauce, prawie i moralności* (On Scientific Knowledge, Law and Morality), Jerzy Licki and Andrzej Kojder, eds. Warsaw: P.W.N.

Piaget, Jean. [1932, in French] 1965. *The Moral Judgment of the Child*. New York: Free Press.

Popper, Karl R. 1971. *The Open Society and its Enemies*. Princeton: Princeton University Press.

_____. 1974. "Scientific Reduction and the Essential Incompleteness of All Science." In Francisco Jose Ayala and Theodosius Dobzhansky, eds., *Studies in the Philosophy of Biology*. Berkeley: University of California Press.

_____. 1979. *Objective Knowledge*. Oxford: Clarendon Press.

Postgate R.W., ed. 1962. *Revolution from 1789 to 1906*. New York: Harper Torchbooks.

Prichard, N.A. 1949. *Moral Obligation*. Oxford: Clarendon Press.

Radbruch, Gustav. [1932] 1950. "Legal Philosophy." In *The Legal Philosophies of Lask, Radbruch and Dabin*, 20th Century Legal Philosophy series, vol. 4. Cambridge, MA: Harvard University Press.

_____. 1963. *Rechtsphilosophie*, 6th ed. Stuttgart: K.F. Koehler.

_____. 1945. "Fünf Minuten Rechsphilosophie." Reprinted in Radbruch 1963.

_____. 1946. "Gesetzliches Unrecht und übergesetzliches Recht." Reprinted in Radbruch 1963.

_____. 1947. "Die Erneuerung des Rechts." In 2 *Die Wandlung*.

_____. 1957. "Der Relativismus in der Rechtsphilosophie." In *Der Mensch im Recht*. Göttingen: Vandenhoeck & Ruprecht.

_____. 1965. *Vorschule der Rechtsphilosophie*. Göttingen: Vandenhoeck & Ruprecht.

Rawls, John. 1971. *A Theory of Justice*. Cambridge, MA: Harvard University Press.

_____. 1993. *Political Liberalism*. New York: Columbia University Press.

Redfield, Robert. 1962. *Human Nature and the Study of Society*. Chicago: University of Chicago Press.

Rescher, Nicholas. 1987. *Ethical Idealism*. Berkeley: University of California Press.

Rest, James R. 1984. "Morality." In Paul H. Mussen, ed., *Handbook of Child Psychology*, vol.3. New York: Wiley.

Riesman, David. 1964. *Abundance For What?* Garden City, NY: Doubleday.

Rokkan, Stein. 1970. *Citizens, Elections, Parties*. Oslo: Universitets Forlaget.

Ross, Alf. 1933. *Kritik der sogenannten praktischen Erkentniss*. Copenhagen.

Ross, W.D. 1930. *The Right and the Good*. Oxford: Clarendon Press.

_____. 1939. *Foundations of Ethics*. Oxford: Clarendon Press.

Russell, Bertrand. 1962. *Human Society in Ethics and Politics*. New York: Mentor Books.

Schachter, Oscar. 1991. *International Law in Theory and Practice*. Dordrecht: Martinus Nijhoff.

Schneider, Hans. 1968. "Das Ermächtigungsgesetz vom 24. Marz 1933." In Gothard Jaspers, ed., *Von Weimar zu Hitler*. Köln: Kiepenhauer & Witsch.

Schwartz, Shalom H. 1977. "Normative Influences on Altruism." 10, *Advances in Experimental Social Psychology*. New York: Academic Press.

_____ and J.A. Howard. 1981. "A Normative Decision-Making Model of Altruism." In J.P. Rushton and R.M. Sorrentino, eds., *Altruism and Helping Behavior: Social, Personality, and Developmental Perspective*. Hillsdale, NJ: Erlbaum.

Selznick, Philip. 1961. "Sociology and Natural Law." 6 *Natural Law Forum*.

Shtromas, Alexander. 1988. "How the End of the Soviet System May Come About." In Alexander Shtromas and Morton A. Kaplan, eds., *The Soviet Union an the Challenge of the Future*, vol. 1. New York: Paragon House Publishers.

Sidgwick, Henry. 1962. *Methods of Ethics*. Chicago: University of Chicago Press.

Sieghart, Paul. 1985. *The Lawful Rights of Mankind*. Oxford: Oxford University Press.

Simmons, Leo W., 1945. *The Role of Aged in Primitive Society*. New Haven: Yale University Press.

Singer, Peter. 1981. *The Expanding Circle*. New York: Farrar, Straus and Giroux.

Stevenson, Charles L. 1963. *Facts and Values*. New Haven: Yale University Press.

Tanaka, Kotaro. 1972. "Some Observations on Peace, Law and Human Rights." In Wolfgang Friedmann, Louis Henkin, and Oliver Lissitzyn, eds., *Transnational Law in a Changing Society*. New York: Columbia University Press.

Tilly, Charles, 1990. "Where do Rights Come From?," 98 *Working Paper of the Center for Studies of Social Change* (prepared for Wilhelm Aubert Memorial Symposium), New York: New School for Social Research.

_____. 1993. *European Revolutions 1492–1992*, Oxford: Blackwell.

Toulmin, Stephen E. 1958. *An Examination of the Place of Reason in Ethics*. Cambridge: Cambridge University Press.

_____. 1982. *The Return to Cosmology*. Berkeley: University of California Press.

Tuck Richard. 1979. *Natural Rights Theories*. Cambridge: Cambridge University Press.

Ulam, Adam. 1994. Review of Daniel Yergin and Thane Gustafson, *Russia 2010: And What it Means for the World*." *The New Republic*, June 20.

VanderWal, Koo. 1990. "Collective Human Rights: A Western View." In Jan Berting and Peter R. Baehr, eds., *Human Rights in a Pluralist World*, Roosevelt Study Center Publication No.10. Westport, CT: Meckler.

Walster, E., E. Berscheid, and G.S. Walster. 1976. "New Directions in Equity Research." In 9, *Advances in Experimental Social Psychology*. New York: Academic Press.

Warnock, G.J. 1967. *Contemporary Moral Philosophy*. New York: St. Martin's Press.

_____. 1971. *The Object of Morality*. London: Methuen.

Weber, Max. [1904-5] 1958. *The Protestant Ethic and the Spirit of Capitalism*. New York: Charles Scribner's Sons.

Wertheimer, Max. 1935. "Some Problems in the Theory of Ethics." 2 *Social Research*.

Wilson, Edward O. 1976. *Sociobiology*. Cambridge, MA: Harvard University Press.

_____. 1978. *On Human Nature*. Cambridge, MA: Harvard University Press.

_____. 1980. "Comparative Social Theory." In *The Tanner Lectures on Human Values*, vol.1. Salt Lake City: University of Utah Press.

_____. 1980. "The Ethical Implications of Human Sociobiology." 10 *Hastings Center Report*.

Wolf, Erik. 1958. "Revolution or Evolution in Gustav Radbruch's Legal Philosophy." 3 *Natural Law Forum*.

_____. 1963. "Gustav Radbruch's Leben und Werk." (Introduction to Radbruch's *Rechtsphilosophie*, 6th. ed.). Stuttgart: K.F. Koehler.

Index